Best wishes Doug Mosl

25 miles
to Torrington

**A history of the
Mash farming family**

25 miles
to Torrington

by Doug Mash

**A history of the
Mash farming family**

First published in 2018 by Hawkes Design & Publishing Ltd.

Copyright © 2018 Hawkes Design & Publishing Ltd – www.hawkesdesign.co.uk

Doug Mash has asserted his moral right to be identified as the author of this work.

ISBN: 978-1-9998335-4-1

CONTENTS

Roots

I often wonder at the way fate seems to decide who we are, where we are, and what we do in life. For example, had it not been for the kindly gesture of a middle-aged Victorian florist, hotel-keeper and greengrocer on a roadside somewhere on the outskirts of London (and opinions vary as to exactly where) I wouldn't be sitting in this ancient cottage in the middle of farming land that has been occupied and worked by my direct descendants for five generations.

Torrington Cottage

The fruit and veg man, whose name was Henry Mash, perhaps wasn't being entirely altruistic when he came to the assistance of a 40-year-old widow called Lucy Austin whose horse and cart had become stuck in a ditch. Henry too was bereaved and after his wife Mary Anne Rose died, the 45-year-old was left in sole care of no less than 15 children. Some were grown up by then, but others weren't, and in fact his poor wife had died in childbirth. In those days, single fathers were rare and the legend is that once he'd helped Mrs Austin from her predicament he said, "I will be back in one year and I will marry you".

And that's exactly what he did, leading to the creation of what we'd term these days a 'blended family' (for Mrs Austin had three of her own children) and the formation of the family business which eventually came to Buckinghamshire: Mash & Austin.

Wedding certificate of Henry Mash & Lucy Austin

It is said that Mrs Austin had plenty of business acumen and helped her new husband ease his way up the social ladder from Brixton, where he ran a florist's, to the smart West End of the city and an undertaking which became one of the major players in fruit and vegetable distribution in London and beyond. Premises were established in Glasshouse Street, Piccadilly (where, to this day, you can still see the letters 'M' and 'A', for Mash & Austin, plus two ornate stone pineapples, on the top of numbers 36-40) and in Long Acre, Covent Garden. There was the establishment of supply chains to hotels, restaurants and, eventually, shipping lines including the most famous of them all: Cunard.

That isn't to say Henry Mash had no business sense of his own. According to legend, Henry's father, Joseph Mash, had left his home in the countryside after his father had asked him to fetch a

Floral display belonging to Henry Mash of Brixton

kettle of water from the nearby spring. Perhaps young Joseph was feeling stubborn, or possibly he was simply being lazy; for whatever reason, an argument ensued and Joseph decided that enough was enough. He made his way to London, married Alice Gunston in 1812 at Islington, and set up home in Clerkenwell, where he ran a potato business in the Goswell Road. I like to think this could be the origin of the 'mashed' potato! In those days, all potatoes were thoroughly washed before they were sold and so the tubers were placed in a large barrel of water, inside which was an arrangement of revolving brushes. A donkey was harnessed to the outside of the barrel and ordered to walk round and round, which turned the brushes and scrubbed the potatoes clean.

In Victorian times it was the case that the larger the town a greengrocery business was located in, the more it needed to specialise in order to stay competitive, hence the early emphasis on potatoes, though it seems the Mash family diversified considerably as the 19th century wore on. Even so, it's easy to understand the initial focus on potatoes in a city where produce was arriving from all parts of the United Kingdom, as well as from the increasing number of countries coming under the British Empire. Typically, a more general retail greengrocery would sell fruit and veg, along with nuts, herbs, dried fruit and flowers, and perhaps the Mash family had more success with this type of business in west London than they might have had in the east of the city; poorer people could rarely afford imported fruit, and so we have the classic Dickensian stories of Victorian children in the East End slums excitedly peeling an orange or cracking a few nuts on Christmas Day.

While it appears that Joseph Mash was a successful businessman, there must have been lean years too, particularly during the Irish Potato Famine of 1845-52, when potatoes were so scarce that even diseased ones held some value; the bad bits were simply cut away and what was left sold at 2.5d. per pound. Despite the ups and downs of the potato trade Joseph Mash still found time to father ten children including the aforementioned Henry, who was born in 1827. Of those who made it beyond childhood (and several didn't, as was usual in those times) some became fruiterers and greengrocers, others went into furniture sales and one, Alice, became a renowned baker. In 1845 she married a German by the name of Johann Wilhelm Heinrich Fuelling - a surname that crops up later in our story. They too had ten children and, as my cousin Susan Bayley found out when she carried out comprehensive and invaluable research into the family tree, the Victorian habit of having big families causes severe problems when you're trying to discover who's who from the past. In fact, Susan came across around 5,000 people with the surname Mash, and because it's a relatively unusual surname it's a possibility we're all related! Plus, when you add regularly reoccurring first names into the mix - all the Henrys and Georges and Williams and Alices and Emilys - you end up with an even bigger headache. So if this narrative becomes confusing, bear with me - I'll try to be as straightforward as I can!

Despite research, we're not entirely sure where the Mash family originates. It's certainly the case that London is its 'home' but Susan Bayley feels that the Mashes could have come from further afield, even as far as Russia, and possibly with Jewish origins. She wonders whether the family might have fled the regular persecutions and pogroms of Jews in the East, and set up home (and business) in London, where there was (and still is, of course) a thriving Jewish community. It might explain the family's skill in business and entrepreneurship, but as there's no concrete proof we'll just have to imagine, or romanticise.

It seems there were definitely Mashes in London at the end of the 18th century, as the following story illustrates. It is taken from an article in the 'Fruit, Flower and Vegetable Trades' Journal', of January 1938, and is about my great-uncle Henry Joseph Mash's Chairmanship of the Worshipful Company of Fruiterers for that year. The writer of the article must have pumped my great-uncle for a few family stories, because this classic is recorded:

"The Mash family has always been intensely loyal to the Crown, but even so one member once went so far as to punch the Prince of Wales on the nose. He drew blood, too.

Years ago the Covent Garden hostelries were not the leather-and-chromium furnished, electric-lighted, highly respectable establishments they are today, but the Covent Gardeners of the day had to take refreshment where they could. Covent Garden, of course, was then almost more renowned as a fashionable and sporting resort than it was as a fruit market, and the inns and coffee houses of the market were a favourite resort of the young 'bucks' of the period. It was whilst one of the early representatives of the Mash family was taking his ease in one of these establishments that there entered a gaily-attired young gallant who, in the manner of the period (when pugilism was ranked highest among all the arts) loudly called the familiar challenge, 'First drop of blood for a bottle of wine!' Young Mash was nothing loth to accept the invitation, and in the good 'mill' punched the gallant's nose to such good effect that he earned not one bottle, but half a dozen. The defeated challenger paid for a bottle of wine with good grace, and this was duly consumed by the two. It was not until after he had departed that the Watch appeared on the scene and the victor was informed that his late combatant was no less illustrious than the Prince of Wales - afterwards King George IV."

Henry Mash

Well, what can I say to the Royal Family other than 'sorry about that' and if we ever meet, the wine is on me!

Henry Joseph Mash (HJ 1st)

Anyway, to continue the story. Henry Mash fathered 15 children (as we've said) including a son, Henry Joseph Mash, who was born in 1850 and is my and Susan Bayley's great-grandfather. In 1869 Henry Joseph Mash (or 'HJ Mash 1st' as we will refer to him) married Georgiana Porter. She was from the Newmarket area and had two brothers, Harry and William James Porter. The latter was in the army and died in South Africa during the first Boer War of 1880-1881. His memory (and his name) lived on in the form of William James Porter ('WJP') Mash (born 1887), one of HJ Mash 1st and Georgina's sons.

HJ 1st and Georgiana had seven other children, and among these were two other significant figures in our story. Aside from WJP Mash (Susan Bayley's grandfather) we have Henry Joseph Mash ('HJ Mash 2nd', known as Harry), born in 1876, and Martin Mash, born in 1880. The latter was my grandfather, and all three were instrumental in making sure that the Mash family business would develop and flourish into the 20th century.

As I mentioned at the beginning, it would appear that the Victorian Mashes were a resourceful lot, not least when it came to keeping up with new trends. As the second half of the 19th century got underway, and Great Britain expanded its interests across the world, there was increased necessity to travel to destinations including India, Africa, Canada and the United States. Steam-powered vessels equipped to carry passengers as well as cargo were becoming faster and more luxurious, and companies including the famous Cunard and White Star lines were springing up to meet the demand.

Of course, passengers and crew had to be fed, and if you were travelling first-class your demands had to be met to the highest standards. During the later part of the century the British Government abolished the duty payable on imported fruit, leading to a greater demand among the better off for top-quality produce. This, and improved refrigeration techniques aboard steamships, meant shipping lines had to offer their passengers the very best if they wanted to retain their business. So from delivering produce to shops, restaurants and hotels in London, Mash & Austin soon joined other wholesalers in supplying ships carrying passengers, crew and cargo across the globe. In 1890 Mash & Austin began to supply the Castle Mail Packets Company, later to merge with the Union Line to become the Union-Castle Steamship Company Ltd. This company's ships, which were mostly named after famous British castles, sailed mainly to India and South Africa, with the occasional voyage to the United States. Shortly after the Cunard Line began regularly to use the Port of London, Mash & Austin were given their first order and an association began which saw M&A supply some of the world's most famous and luxurious cruise liners.

Perhaps it was this that got the Mash family thinking about growing and selling their own produce, instead of being middlemen for other growers. Maybe it was for other reasons. The basis for the decision is lost in the mists of time, but it is certainly the case that by the end of the 19th Century Henry Joseph Mash 1st and his young sons, who would become the mainstays of the family business, were looking beyond London towards parcels of agricultural land that would provide for all their fruit and vegetable growing needs.

CHAPTER 2

The Making of Torrington Farm

Unlike the Lake District, Snowdonia or the Pennines, the Chiltern Hills around Buckinghamshire don't really shout loudly about themselves. There isn't much in the way of craggy peaks or stomach-turning drops into sweeping, picturesque valleys. The beauty of the Chilterns is more subtle; ancient woodlands and gentle chalk grasslands, ponds, streams and all varieties of wildlife combine to create a peaceful, reflective and lush landscape that, until relatively recently, had barely changed at all for hundreds of years. Even now, when rush hour is finished and everyone has gone to work or school, it's hard to believe that the area around Chesham (close to where the Mash family farm is situated) is only 25 miles from the centre of London.

Chesham in the Chiltern Hills, just 25 miles from London

Perhaps it was that fact which first attracted HJ Mash 1st and his sons to this area. Setting off early, a horse and cart laden with produce could feasibly get to Covent Garden and back in a day. But in Victorian times there were still plenty of areas much closer to the city that had not yet been built over, and were still used for agricultural purposes.

By Order of the Trustees.

Grove Lane Farm

AND

WOODEN BABYLON,

NEAR

CHESHAM, BUCKS,

Between two and three miles from Chesham, on the Metropolitan Railway, and between three and four from Great Berkhamstead and Boxmoor, on the L. & N. W. Railway, and on the road leading from Boxmoor to Chesham.

PARTICULARS AND CONDITIONS OF SALE

OF THE VALUABLE

FREEHOLD ESTATE,

KNOWN AS

GROVE LANE FARM AND WOODEN BABYLON,

COMPRISING

A COMPACT FREEHOLD FARM,

With Farm-house, ample Outbuildings, and containing an area of

29 acres **1** rood **33** poles

Of VALUABLE PASTURE and ARABLE LAND,

The greater part planted with Well-matured and Thriving Fruit Trees forming Excellent Orchards ; also

EIGHT COTTAGES,

Brick Erected and Tiled,

With Outbuildings and a small enclosure of Pasture Land,

Which will be Sold by Auction, in One Lot, by

MESSRS. HUMBERT, SON & FLINT

By order of the Trustees of the Will of the late Mr. Joseph Barnes,

At the Town Hall, Chesham,

On Wednesday, 26th day of August, 1896, at 3 o'clock precisely.

Particulars and Conditions of Sale may be obtained of Messrs. Francis & How, Solicitors, Chesham ; or of the Auctioneers, at Watford, Herts, and 11, Serle Street, Lincoln's Inn, London, W.C.

T. J. PEACOCK, PRINTER, CHESHAM.

Notice of Sale, Grove Lane Farm

Ashley Green Village, little has changed over the decades

So if geographical distance wasn't the sole attraction, then what else was? Well, it could be that the Chilterns' long history of fruit-growing and orchard cultivation was a primary reason. The area was particularly well-known for its cherries, picked by parties of workers travelling from London and other large conurbations nearby, and used in gin and other spirits. There was also vegetable growing, in particular cauliflowers, peas and beans. Insofar as the Mash family viewed it, there was potential to grow both fruit and vegetables, and diversify as and when the market demanded.

In 1896, it came to the attention of the Mash family that a 'compact freehold farm' had come up for sale in Grove Lane, in the parish of Ashley Green, just outside the town of Chesham. The farm was known as Grove Lane Farm, comprising '29 acres, 1 rood and 33 poles'. A rood is equivalent to a quarter of an acre, while a pole was five-and-a-half yards. You don't hear much about such measurements these days!

The estate also included a farmhouse and outbuildings, eight cottages, pasture and arable land planted with 'well-matured and thriving fruit trees forming excellent orchards.' There is also the mention of 'Wooden Babylon', which was a dwelling (or possibly several dwellings) that appeared to accommodate itinerant farm workers and/or gypsies and other travellers. The sale of the land and buildings was held at Chesham Town Hall on August 26th, 1896, and was on behalf of the trustees of the will of the late Joseph Barnes, whose family had had the land for at least 100 years

Workmen building Orchard Leigh Villas, late 19th century

previously, according to title deeds from the 18th century still in our possession. It wasn't the

Orchard Leigh Villas completed in 1898

biggest parcel of land by any means, but it was enough to establish and grow an agricultural business.

Sadly, we have no record of how much Grove Lane Farm and Wooden Babylon sold for. Suffice to say that HJ Mash 1st and his sons successfully purchased it and were soon up and running in terms of farming the land. Along Grove Lane, opposite the farm, stood a smart country house of the late Victorian period. History records that it was occupied by Sir Frederick Dunbar and was called Torrington House. Today, of course, the Mash family farm is called 'Torrington Farm' but whether the name was changed from 'Grove Lane Farm' to Torrington Farm in order to match its neighbour, or 'Torrington' was adopted for another reason, we do not know. At any rate it seems the farm's name was changed fairly quickly after its purchase, possibly to avoid confusion with another farm, also up the lane, called Little Grove. This (and, subsequently, its near-neighbour, Grove Farm) was purchased by the Harman family not long after the Mashes came to Grove Lane and, like us, the Harmans are still there to this day.

So Torrington Farm it became, and by 1899 some of the family were living in and around Grove Lane, including a George Fuelling, who must have been the son of the German-born Johann Wilhelm Heinrich Fuelling and who married a Mash, Alice, in 1875. That George's mother was also called Alice Mash (at least before her marriage) must have seemed slightly odd, but in those days the habit of marriage between cousins was by no means uncommon, and the Mash family were no exception.

And what of 'Wooden Babylon'? Well, if the place was occupied by sinners living in roughly-constructed shacks, as the name suggests, it seems to have been transformed into a small collection of Victorian 'villas', as they were called then - today we'd term them 'semi's' - which were collectively titled 'Orchard Leigh', and located just around the corner from Grove Lane. Soon after the First World War, the largest of these villas was turned into a health sanatorium by an American health guru by the name of Bernarr Macfadden. In those days, so-called 'nature cures' involving large amounts of fresh air and exercise were all the rage, especially among the

Bernarr MacFadden's Orchard Leigh Healthatorium, which led to Champneys Health Resort, Tring

Bernarr MacFadden's Orchard Leigh Healthatorium,

progressive middle-class, and Macfadden obviously considered the lovely countryside around Orchard Leigh the ideal place for stressed urbanites to unwind in nature. Well, some business ideas never change!

One of Macfadden's close associates was Russian-born Stanley Lief, who had graduated from Macfadden's health training school in the United States. Lief had been a poorly child whose parents had moved to South Africa in order that he could live in a healthier, warmer climate. As a teenager, Lief came across a magazine in which Macfadden had written about the benefits of his own 'Nature Cure' and was so

Stanley Lief's Nature Cure Resort at Tring, which became the famous Champneys business

impressed that he followed the article's instructions to the letter, with the result that he became a total convert to its benefits. When Macfadden opened Orchard Leigh as a nature cure centre, he asked Lief to run the place day-to-day. He did so until the establishment moved to

Champneys, near Tring, Hertfordshire, and Lief moved with it, running the new resort very successfully for 20 years. To this day, Champneys is an internationally-famous brand in the field of health and well-being.

In the very early days of Torrington Farm, horses were the singular most popular form of farm 'machinery' and, as we've mentioned, took the produce grown on the farm to London by cart, returning in the evening with excrement both animal and human, collected from mews and middens across the city and used as fertiliser. And while chemical fertilisers were being used in late Victorian times, it would seem that the Mashes were still using traditional methods, at least at first, and rather successfully too. In his book, 'Seventy Summers' (BBC Publications, 1986) the late Tony Harman, my farming neighbour up Grove Lane, refers to the fact that the Mashes farm "was run on very traditional lines, using little chemical manure." He also mentions that the failure of another nearby farmer, one Mr Ford, who had used chemicals extensively, was interpreted by older people thereabouts as "a failure of science. Mr Ford had gone bankrupt, or nearly so, because the artificial fertilisers had poisoned his land and the tractors had ruined the

Horses were once the main form of farm 'machinery' (Mr Chapman, ploughman of Lye Green)

21

Steam wagon driven by Mr Reid in 1917

drainage on it, whereas Mr Mash, keeping on with his traditional methods of using animal manure and horse-drawn implements, was obeying the laws of nature and survived."

As Tony Harman goes on to say, the truth wasn't quite a simple as that, but it is a fact that the agricultural world the Mashes had bought into was changing rapidly. A horse could plough an acre a day, so the 29 acres purchased by the Mashes would have seemed manageable at first, particularly to a family inexperienced at farming. But advances in steam power, as we have looked at with regard to faster ships crossing the world's oceans to every corner of Empire, were being scaled down to accommodate changes at a more domestic level. The traction engine was seen more and more in the countryside, particularly at ploughing and harvesting time, and was also used as a stationary vehicle for jobs such as threshing. The age of the horse - which, in reality, was still in evidence until after the Second World War - was ending, albeit slowly.

As we've seen in our own times - and in our own business at Torrington Farm - increasing mechanisation leads to fewer workers being required on the land. That may have also been the case in late 19th and early 20th century Buckinghamshire, but steam engines and other new-fangled methods of farming didn't appear to have impacted upon the Mash habit of hiring large

Mash & Austin letterhead showing properties acquired

136-138 Lye Green Road

numbers of local people - some full-time, some casual - to work on the farm. Or, more correctly, farms, because by 1921, just 25 years since the Mashes had arrived in Grove Lane, four other farms had been acquired, including Lye Green (1909), Brockhurst Farm (1914), Whelpley Ash Farm and Pockets Dell (1920), and Moors Farm (1921). Evidently, the Mashes were an ambitious lot, and needed much more than the initial 29 acres to meet the demands from the London fruit and vegetable markets and the shipping lines. With 500-plus acres came the demand for farm managers, ploughmen, planters, pickers, packers and a whole host of other tasks associated with a flourishing agri-business.

Fortunately, there was a population large enough around the Chesham area to meet the demand. As anyone from the area knows, the town is famous for its four 'B's': Beer, Brushes, Boots and Baptists. At the time the Mashes arrived there were two breweries in the town - How's and Chesham Brewery - and more than 80 pubs serving a population of 9,000. Brush-making

BEER: The old brewery on White Hill and a bottle label from Chesham & Brackley Breweries

BRUSHES: Beechwood's factory in Higham Road

was long-established in the town by 1895 and as the UK's centre of the industry had no less than 12 brushmaking firms. It's thought that brushmaking began as a result of a large number of beech trees in the area, which attracted woodworkers making shovels and spades. In those days little went to waste, so brushes were made from offcuts and an industry sprang up. As for boots, the town had at least 10 factories in operation at the turn of the 19th century, supplying boots to the military and other uniformed services as well as farm and industrial workers. By all accounts Chesham's trees not only supplied the brush-

BOOTS: Newton's factory in Townsend Road

BAPTISTS: An early Chapel in Chesham Broadway

Chesham Cricket Club, early 20th Century (①Mr Giffard Newton, Senior ②Martin Mash)

Martin Mash

making industry but provided the tannin needed to break down and animal hides into leather. One of the best-known boot manufacturers in the town was Giffard Newton and Sons, and it was Giffard Newton Jnr who, alongside my grandfather Martin Mash, was a mainstay of Chesham Cricket Club for many years. Giffard was my mum's cousin.

The Baptist part of the four B's stems from the fact that Chesham has a long history of non-conformity. John Wesley preached in the town and the first Baptists met in the middle of the 17th century. There were several Baptist chapels in Chesham and various branches in the surrounding areas, no doubt providing comfort and refreshment for the more godly people who weren't in one of the 80 pubs!

So there was no shortage of 'hands', as they were termed, to maintain and develop the Mash family farms. In turn, the family acquired, or built from new, a whole range of cottages for lease to farm managers, their families and workers who were employed full-time. This accommodation was guaranteed for life and at the time of writing we still have one former employee, 89-year-old Don Dell, exercising his right to remain in his home which was laid down so many years ago. If nothing else, the Mash family has always been considered a fair employer that took care of its workers, and I'm very pleased we're upholding that tradition to this day.

Chesham Cricket Club, 1947 (①Jack Mash ②Giffard Newton ③George Piggin)

CHAPTER 3

A Murder Mystery

In the very last year of the 19th century Henry Mash died, followed by his wife, Lucy Austin, just a few months later. The fruiterer and florist who, by the very act of rescuing a damsel in distress in a ditch, had started a flourishing retail and wholesale business lived long enough to see the purchase of Torrington Farm and the expansion of the Mash business from London into Buckinghamshire.

Whatever business interests Henry Mash still had in Mash & Austin now transferred wholly to his son, Henry Joseph 1st, and HJ's sons Harry, Martin and Will. We're fairly sure that at this point the farming side of the business became known as HJ Mash Ltd, while the Mash & Austin name carried on in London.

Milk bottles given to Doug by Sandra Carter, daughter of Jesse Dell

In 1911 a dairy was built at Lye Green farm and the family diversified into milk production. I have two old milk bottles which reside in the office at Torrington Farm; one is 'the property of HJ Mash Ltd', while the other, younger example, belongs to 'WJ and M Mash Ltd' reflecting a split which took place in the company in the mid 1930s. At some stage very late in the 19th century HJ 1st also acquired a property in Cookham, Berkshire, called Winter Hill Farm. This was also close to the village of Little Marlow, and it would be here that another outlet of the Mash family business would be established. At this time there were various properties in London, and outside of it, that were owned or leased by the Mash family and it was at one of these, Lambridge House, in Henley-on-Thames, that one of the strangest episodes in the family's history occurred.

We must turn the clock back to 1893, just

three years before the farm at Chesham was purchased. Lambridge House was leased by HJ 1st, who used it as a weekend and summer retreat. HJ 1st employed a housekeeper by the name of Kate Dungey, a 30-year-old woman who was, by various accounts, very attractive. She was unmarried, and lived alone in the house except for two young boys named Froome who tended to sleep there in the evenings.

On December 8, James Froome, the eldest of the two, went home for his tea then, with his younger brother Harry in tow, made his way to Lambridge House. They knocked at the door as usual, but received no reply. Making their way around the back, the boys saw there was a candle burning in the kitchen. They shouted Miss Dungey's name several times but there was no answer. One of the boys heard a strange noise coming from the nearby woods which 'sounded like a cat growling at a mouse.'

Terrified and bewildered, the boys ran home and called their father. He in turn went to fetch George Dawson, a foreman who worked for HJ 1st, and they all went back to Lambridge House to see if they could locate Miss Dungey. They managed to enter the house and at first, nothing seemed to be amiss. Kate's knitting was where it had been that afternoon and two cups and saucers had been laid for tea. But after lighting a candle they noticed bloodstains on the wall and the floor. In addition Miss Dungey's dogs were nowhere to be found.

Taking a lantern, they searched the woods and quickly found Miss Dungey's body on the ground. She had been savagely beaten to death with a rammer, a tool used to mash pig food. Still in her grip was a fireside poker - there had obviously been a hell of a fight. Dawson and Froome left the body alone, and took a cab to Henley police station where they reported the murder. The police returned with them and on inspection of the body found multiple and deep wounds, some to the bone.

Several days later there was an inquest at Henley and, as was usual then, all the gory details came out in the local press. HJ 1st attended, telling the jury that Miss Dungey was 'one of the most innocent creatures that ever breathed, of an excellent disposition, and pure-minded…a most valuable servant'. Mr Mash offered a £100 reward to find the killer, and very soon suspicion fell on Dawson's brother-in-law, one Walter Rathall, who had worked for HJ 1st but had left under something of a cloud. He had been seen around Lambridge House in the days leading up to the murder and a month after the incident he was arrested in Daventry.

Rathall had to be protected from a baying mob when he arrived at Reading Magistrates' Court on January 11, 1894. As the trial progressed it was learned that Rathall, who was acquainted with Miss Dungey, was lodging in Henley on the day of the murder and had left his house that afternoon - clutching a three-foot long stick - and hadn't returned until 7.45pm. The following day, his landlady asked him if he had had any involvement in the death, which he denied, saying he could never hurt such a 'poor creature'.

There was also evidence that Miss Dungey and Mr Dawson had 'history', in that they'd argued some time previously about who should occupy Lambridge House. It seems that Dawson had occupied it at one stage, but had been replaced by Miss Dungey and it appeared he rather resented this.

Nevertheless, witnesses including James Froome, one of the boys who had originally looked for Miss Dungey, testified to seeing Rathall in the area of Lambridge House around the time of the murder. Things weren't looking at all good for Rathall as the case headed towards its conclusion and no doubt those who were watching from the public gallery had visions of Rathall swinging from a rope.

All this certainty stopped when George Smith, the surgeon who examined Miss Dungey's body, told the court that the injuries could have been caused by a woman. Hard on the heels of this was new evidence by George Dawson, who claimed to have witnessed an argument the previous summer between Miss Dungey and HJ 1st's wife, Georgiana. It appeared that Mrs Mash had threatened to hit Miss Dungey with an umbrella, the argument becoming so serious that HJ 1st had to intervene. These two speculative comments, particularly the latter, weren't taken too seriously by the magistrates, but there was also the fact that no blood was found on Rathall's clothes, and that bootprints at the murder scene didn't match those of his boots.

There seemed little to conclusively connect Rathall with the murder - and certainly no motive - and at the end of the trial the defendant was acquitted due to lack of evidence. Although HJ 1st doubled the reward money, no-one else was ever arrested or even questioned about Miss Dungey's death, leaving it a mystery to this day. A much fuller version of the events can be found in an excellent book by Elizabeth J. Hazeldine called 'The Wilful Murder of Kate Laura Dungey'.

There is an interesting postscript to this story, in that none other than Henry Joseph Mash 2nd married Kate Dungey's sister Helena in 1900. It is assumed that the Dungey and Mash families knew each prior to the murder, because Miss Dungey's father Walter was a fruit-grower from Kent and it is almost certain that HJ 1st and Walter had done business together. The marriage of HJ 1st's eldest son and Helena Dungey took place at Goudhurst, in Kent, and we have a photograph of the event. HJ 1st and his wife Georgiana are standing at the back, along with Walter and Ellen Dungey. I'm sure it must have been an occasion for celebration, but I also can't help thinking that poor murdered Kate couldn't have been far from the guests' thoughts that day.

HJ 2nd and his new wife settled into accommodation in Garrick Street, Covent Garden. They were married for almost 60 years, until Helena's death in 1957, and enjoyed a seemingly happy

Wedding of HJ 2ⁿᵈ and Helena Dungey (sister of murdered Kate)
① *HJ 1ˢᵗ* ② *HJ 2ⁿᵈ* ③ *Helena Dungey* ④ *Walter Dungey* ⑤ *Georgina Mash*
⑥ *William J Mash* ⑦ *Martin Mash*

life, travelling the world aboard some of the great cruise liners of the time. The murder, however, was barely spoken of, if at all. My relations Richard and Anthony Mash, great-grandsons of HJ 1ˢᵗ and Georgiana, recall only finding out about the incident when one of them asked about a portrait of Kate which was in the family's possession. We were all vaguely aware that something untoward had happened but it wasn't discussed in depth and we never knew the full details until after the deaths of HJ 2ⁿᵈ and his wife. Certainly, HJ 1ˢᵗ and his wife left Lambridge House for good following the murder, purchasing the aforementioned Winter Hill Farm and retaining other properties in Henley.

Back to farming, and while the Mash business was starting to flourish around the turn of the 19ᵗʰ century, the picture elsewhere was nowhere near as rosy. As we've said, mechanisation and increasing urbanisation, plus a run of bad harvests from the 1880s onwards, meant that the English countryside was changing beyond recognition. Many families who had worked on the land for centuries found employment opportunities shrinking, and were forced to move into the cities - or abroad, to the colonies and America - to gain work. Cottage industries that supported the rural economy also collapsed as industrialisation speeded up manufacturing tenfold and more.

In a way, the Mash family were also part of this new way of doing things and yet, ironically, when the bad times really hit the British economy in the late 1920s and '30s our business was on such a sure footing that we continued to be profitable and were able to take on workers, as opposed to laying people off. A lot of this I put down to the way our acres, particularly our orchards, were planted and managed. Our business supplying hotels, restaurants and wholesale markets in London, plus the deliveries to the ports of Southampton and Liverpool, required us to be as efficient as possible, and the traditional way orchards were operated in England - that is, in a rather haphazard way, without a great deal of planning - simply wouldn't suit a business like ours.

Instead, it was decided that many trees of the same variety would be grown; in orderly rows, harvested at the same time, graded and taken to market. Varieties included Bramley Seedlings, Lanes' Prince Albert and Worcester Permains. These were apples that were relatively new to the scene in 1900, but were gaining in popularity. Now, of course, such 'traditional' British varieties face stiff competition from apples produced abroad, particularly varieties from New Zealand and Australia. Not only that, but the traditional method of growing tall apple trees has disappeared too. As my late neighbour, Tony Harman, said in '*Seventy Summers*': "Little trees, just a few feet high, have been bred, which can be picked from the ground and which grow fruit of a completely uniform size, exactly what the supermarket buyer wants so that he can provide the same thing for his customers via cold store throughout the season."

How true, and it was for that reason, among others, that we eventually got rid of our orchards in the early 1980s. But that's a story for later on!

By 1900, Torrington House itself was occupied by Alice Mash, the daughter of Henry Mash and the sister of HJ 1st, and her husband George Fuelling, who was also related to her. We know this through the research done by Susan Bayley, and from a most interesting book called '*Thoresby to Torrington*', by an American writer, Valerie Stern, whose paternal grandmother's family was called Brown, and came from Nottinghamshire. Mrs Stern carried out eight years of research before she wrote her book, which she 'novelised' so that it reads as a story rather than a list of facts. Her research focused on one Harry Brown, born in 1844 in Nottinghamshire and reputedly the illegitimate son of Viscount Newark. His young and poor mother was sent away in shame, leaving Harry to be brought up by his grandparents. At 16, he joined the army and saw service across the world, including in India, Ireland, Egypt and Gibraltar, attaining the rank of Sergeant.

Harry Brown married Lucy Street in 1871 and the couple produced 12 children. Mr Brown eventually retired from the army, took a job with the Cunard Line as a Superintendent of stewards and moved his family to Liverpool.

It was there that he met HJ 1st, as a result of mutual business interests and a shared passion for horse-racing. They became firm friends, and in 1899 met up at the funeral of a poultry dealer who had a large contract with Cunard. According to Mrs Stern's account, HJ 1st expressed sympathy with Mr Brown, whose young daughter Marjorie had died in the early part of that year from pneumonia. He invited the Browns to stay at their house, Winter Hill Farm, for a weekend, and at the end of their visit (in April 1900) he mentioned that his sister and her husband had a house to rent, and would they be interested?

They were, and so HJ 1st took them to Torrington House to meet Alice and George. They, in turn, took the Browns across the road to Torrington Cottage - which is where I'm currently living. The pair were taken by the place - and not surprisingly, as it's beautiful - and decided to lease it as a weekend retreat. Mr and Mrs Brown and their children spent several happy summers

Torrington Cottage, mid 20th Century

The Brown family, who came to live at Torrington House

there and in 1907, took over the lease of Torrington House when George and Alice Fuelling decided to move back to Kensington. The lure of a bigger space for the family - albeit one that was getting married and moving away - was great and so they took it, enjoying weekends and summers there until they moved down from Liverpool full time around 1913. Harry and Lucy Brown died in 1925 and 1934 respectively, and are both buried at St John's churchyard in Ashley Green cemetery, not far from Torrington Farm and the area they loved. Their daughter, Joyce, married indirectly into the Mash family when she wed John James 'Jack' Richmond in 1919. Jack was the brother of Nellie and Lilian Richmond, sisters who married WJP Mash (Susan Bayley's grandfather) and Martin Mash (my grandfather) respectively. Jack Richmond came to work for us and was farmer manager here for many years, thus continuing the Mash tradition of keeping it in the family!

Mr Harry Brown and Betty Richmond, his grandaughter (the daughter of Joyce)

CHAPTER 4

Going Further Afield

As we've mentioned, the early years of the 20th Century were a time of great prosperity for the Mash family business and even during the First World War, when many local lads who'd laboured on the farms were sent off to fight (many never returning, of course). The demand for food was so high that agricultural businesses like ours were turning over large sums of money.

For example, the accounts filed for the year ending September 30, 1918 (less than two months before the Great War would finish) show a turnover of £48,922 - more than £3 million in today's money. The profit on this was almost £9,000, equivalent to more than £500,000 today.

HJ 2nd at Winter Hill Farm

Perhaps it's no wonder, then, that when the opportunity came to purchase more land in the Little Marlow area, the family jumped at it. In December 1918 an auction was held to dispose of the Little Marlow Estate, which included the manor house, a grand mansion called Westhorpe House, numerous other farms, cottages, a pub, a post office, woods, plantations, fields and allotments. HJ 2nd's connections with Winter Hill Farm, which overlooks the estate, meant that the family couldn't fail to be interested in the disposal of the estate.

HJ 2nd purchased eight cottages in the village, at a total of £1, 470 (£92,000 in today's money - a bargain!!) plus the 219-acre Little Marlow Farm, which comprised an eight-bedroomed farmhouse and a whole raft of farm buildings including barns, cowsheds and pigstys, plus the acres of arable and pasture land. Just the job for an expanding agricultural business. The main prize of the sale, however, was the 'imposing Early Georgian Mansion known as Westhorpe House' (according to the brochure, which is still in the possession of Richard Mash, HJ 2nd's grandson). The house and grounds occupied 115 acres and had been built around 1700 for James Chase MP, though it is thought there was another property previously on the site which had been destroyed by fire. The house had been purchased in 1809 by Field Marshal Sir George Nugent and at the time of sale in 1918 was occupied by another army officer, Major Herbert Gordon.

Westhorpe House had 12 main bedrooms plus five servants' rooms, a large kitchen garden, stabling, parkland, two cottages and all the trappings that a wealthy gentleman of the period could ever wish for. In short, that gentleman was HJ Mash 2nd and he was very keen to purchase it. However, for whatever reason Westhorpe House failed to make its reserve price of £14,000

Westhorpe House - a family gathering

(£876,000 in today's money) and was withdrawn from sale. But not for long..... at some stage soon after the auction HJ 2nd finally purchased it and so it came into the family's possession, remaining there for almost 50 years.

Richard Mash and his brother, Anthony, lived at the house as boys, and remember the place as rambling, but somewhat dilapidated:

"It was a good place to live," recalled Anthony. "There were about 42 rooms in total, so it was a large house and you certainly weren't tripping over each other! We used to climb up on the roof and take potshots at the squirrels living in the trees.

"When we lived there, the days of Westhorpe being full of servants were long gone, and that was the problem: the house was dilapidated and the upkeep of it was huge. Very little had been done inside since our grandfather had purchased it, and I remember a very interesting selection of fungi growing out of the walls right at the bottom of the house!

"The house had been burned down at least once, if not two or three times, and we were told that one of the signatories to Charles I's execution had lived on the site. During the First World War the Second Battalion The Lancashire Fusiliers were billeted here before their embarkation to France. The rifle racks they installed in the old dairy could still be seen when we were boys.

"When the old man (HJ 2nd, Richard and Anthony's grandfather) died in 1968 the decision was made to get rid of the house. We were grown up then and away so we weren't party to it. It was sold to the local authority, Wycombe District Council, and was to be the centrepiece of a public country park. Well, we're still waiting for that to happen! It was a grandiose idea, but financially not viable at all. It was later sold to Lexmark, who were there until about 2004. There's a bloody great modern carbuncle on the back of it now, and I believe the plan is to create around 30 apartments in there and the main house. I don't think there would be much objection to that; anything's better than it remaining empty."

The area around Little Marlow purchased by the Mash family included many acres of fruit trees with a very high yield, and at some stage in the early 20th century a jam factory was established in the area to preserve and bottle this fruit. Richard and Anthony have seen Kilner-style jars with 'Mash & Austin' stamped on their bottom, so it might be the case that at one time we had our own-branded jam, though I can't find much more evidence for this. It was to Little Marlow that Mash cattle were driven from the Chesham area farms, the drovers stopping at the Magpies pub, half way between Chesham and Little Marlow, so that a new set of drovers could lead the cattle the rest of the way. Soberly, of course!

As well as Little Marlow Farm and Westhorpe House, the immediate post-war years also saw the purchase of farms at Whelpley Hill and Pockets Dell, near Chesham. The former was on

Excerpt from the farm wages book 1917

land owned by the Constable Curtis family, who resided in The Hall, Berkhamsted. At that time, several local landowners were disposing of estates, or parts thereof, as a result of a downturn in the farming business. But as we've said, against all trends the Mash business was on a much surer footing at this time.

Henry Joseph Mash 1st died in 1919, leaving the companies of HJ Mash Ltd and Mash & Austin Ltd to his sons HJ 2nd, WJP (Will) and Martin Mash, plus property in Henley to his daughter Eleanor, property in London to his daughter May, a house in Cookham to his daughter Annie,

Funeral of HJ Mash 1st at Cookham Dean

Mash staff in front of the old packing shed, approx 1934

property in Maidenhead to his sister Minnie, and, to his 'faithful servants' William and Daisy Pheby cottages in Cookham Dean and Bourne End.

In addition, there were legacies of up to £100 (around £6,000 in today's money) for various brothers, sisters, cousins and former servants. The Mash sons also inherited the houses at Orchard Leigh, along with everything else connected with the business. When Georgiana Mash followed her husband to the grave in 1921, her legacies were somewhat more domestic, and included jewellery, clothing and furniture which went variously to daughters, sons, daughters-in-law and grandchildren.

As we've said, the Little Marlow property was occupied by Henry Joseph 1st's eldest son, HJ 2nd (Harry) who

Spraying the orchards, 1930s

Orchard spraying 1930s

Apple packing shed; apples being graded

Trenches dug to install spray lines

Pump for chemicals to the orchards

Barrells of tar oil and sulphur

looked after the business there. My own grandfather, Martin Mash, took care of the trade in London, while Will (WJP) Mash oversaw the farms around Chesham. By all accounts the latter was a good employee, inspiring loyalty among his workers including local families such as the Fosketts, the Dells and

Storage of apples in straw

the Puddephatts (the latter seems to be spelled various ways, according to who's spelling it!), several generations of whom are associated with the Mash business in this area. In 1918, for example, the wage bill was £3,691, close on £250,000 in today's money, and we were employing people full-time, part-time and seasonally. Manpower was needed during the 1920s and 30s,

Mash & Austin vehicles (1) *Jack Richmond* (2) *Will Mash* (3) *Bramley Mash* (4) *Ernest Bucknell*

certainly, but the business also required a high level of technological investment in order to meet demand, particularly from the cruise ships which were then in their heyday. About 20 years after they were planted and had reached maturity, spray lines were put down in the orchards to combat pests and fungi. In those days the apples would have been picked with a 20-rung ladder; when my turn came to manage the farm a 40-rung equivalent was needed, which shows just how quickly they'd grown. The orchards were big - around 200 acres - and while the traditional method of storing apples (involving the fruit being packed in layers of straw and laid down in barns) was employed at first, it soon became clear that a more up-to-date means was needed to keep up with the demands of the ships.

The Mash family were one of the first farmers in the area - if not the first - to introduce gas-powered cold storage for

A Frigidaire magazine advert featuring the Mash's business

keeping the fruit. The cold stores were about 30ft square and some 20ft high. They were installed by the Frigidaire company, who serviced them every three months or so, and all the boxes of fruit were stored at various levels right up to the top of the store. We were also one of the first farms to bringing in a grading system for apples according to size. The retail firm, restaurant or ship's kitchen would ask for the size they'd need and the fruit would be individually wrapped in paper before being sent off to market, or to the docks.

And no longer was it horse and cart, laden with produce and plodding along country lanes, conveying the produce to London. After the First World War the lorry began to dominate Britain's roads and by the 1930s the horse, while still seen around farms, was consigned to much more local and domestic duties. Unsurprisingly, the Mash business acquired a fleet of lorries to service their customers and at one stage during the 1930s we had about 15 of these, plus numerous farm vehicles and various pieces of plant and machinery. A list of vehicles repaired and maintained at Torrington Farm during 1933, 1934 and 1935 includes Ford, Sunbeam, Humber, Austin and Morris vehicles (the latter four are great but long-since-departed names from the early days of British motor manufacturing, of course), milk vans, sludge lorries, tractors, threshing machines, ploughs and spraying pumps. The trucks and the gas-powered cold stores (which were later electrified) meant the Mash business could supply fruit all year round, not just seasonally. This gave us a big advantage over our rivals because we could command the market, particularly for the cruise ships, for 12 months of the year.

The net profits from the years 1918-1930 reflect this. A couple of losses were recorded - history does not tell us exactly why, though they do coincide with the purchase of farms at the above-mentioned Pockets Dell and Whelpley Ash, plus another at Moors Farm - but on the whole, the accounts for the period look very healthy, with a total of £32,000 (almost £2 million) for the 12-year period. Even into the 1930s, and the start of the Great Depression, the accounts remained healthy and yet, underneath the success certain problems were manifesting themselves. In the ledger which records the annual directors' meetings for the period, the entry for December 5th, 1933, under the heading 'Little Marlow Farm', reads like this:

Display of Mash fruit and veg heading for a local show

'Mr WJP Mash pointed out that with six farms to work at Chesham, his time to administer Little Marlow Farm was restricted, and suggested that it would be as well if Mr HJ Mash would take over and control the working of that farm, say at the commencement of the next financial year, i.e. 1st April 1934.

Mr HJ Mash expressed his willingness to this arrangement provided that Mr WJP Mash and Mr Martin Mash would work in conjunction with him when necessary.

They both agreed to this and it was resolved that the foregoing arrangements be made and adhered to next year.'

In a ledger which almost exclusively dwells on the mundane, day-to-day operations of a large business, this understated yet significant paragraph strikes me as very interesting. Was there some dispute or disillusionment at the way the operation at Little Marlow Farm was being run, and is there some inference that HJ 2nd wasn't quite pulling his weight there? At all the other meetings

Orchards in blossom

of the period, at least up until 1936, nothing else of a similar nature was said (the business for discussion going back to usual matters including the purchase of Scammell trucks, directors' dividends and the rent on various cottages) but WJP Mash obviously felt strongly enough about something that was happening - or, perhaps more accurately, not happening - to allow such a statement to be put on record. As we now know, it was quite possibly a foreshadowing of events later on in the 1930s which prompted a dramatic split in the family firm.

CHAPTER 5

A Fork in the Road

O n Thursday June 15, 1936, the directors of HJ Mash Ltd (which comprised HJ 2nd, Martin and Will Mash) gathered at 36 Glasshouse Street, London, for what would turn out to be an extraordinary directors' meeting.

The main business of the day is worth quoting in full, as it was taken down by the company secretary, Mr E.J. Bucknell:

The business of the dissolution of the Company and the division of the properties was discussed, and it was finally resolved that HJ Mash esq. should acquire the properties of the company at Little Marlow, viz Little Marlow Farm and various cottages, Westhorpe premises and park, Bloom and Warren Woods and Winchbottom together with the live and dead stock thereat as valued at 31st of March 1936, all standing in the Company's books at that date @ £24,502.10.10.

WJP Mash esq. and Martin Mash esq. to acquire jointly as their share the remaining properties at Chesham, viz:

Torrington Farm, Lye Green Farm, Brockhurst Farm, Whelpley Ash Farm, Moors Farm, Orchard Leigh and stores and sheds, together with the live and dead stock thereat, all standing in the company's books as at March 31st 1936 at £43,611.16.3.

As the total value of the Chesham and Marlow properties amounted to £68,114.7.1 the one third share taken by each shareholder viz £22,704.15.8 would be £1,797.15.2 under the value of the Marlow properties acquired by HJ Mash esq. and it was agreed that he should repay the other two shareholders by this amount of £1,797.15.2

In regard to the loans against the company it was agreed that the total amount should be apportioned equally between the three shareholders, i.e. each to take over one third of the bank loan and overdraft and Mash & Austin Ltd. loan.

The dissolution of the company on the foregoing basis to be as from 1st April 1936. The book value of properties to be verified by the auditors. Proposed by Mr WJP Mash, seconded by Mr Martin Mash and carried unanimously.

So there it was. After many years trading, the firms of HJ Mash Ltd and Mash & Austin would be dissolved and the grandsons of Henry Mash would go their separate ways. Exactly why is not known; as in the last chapter, we can only speculate on possible resentment at someone not pulling their weight. However, it seems that all parties agreed to the dissolution of the company with little or no obvious dissent, and I and my cousins Richard and Anthony Mash recall that in later years, there seemed to be no personal animosity between the brothers and their families.

On June 30th, 1936, another meeting of the directors was held, this time in the London office of Morgan Bros, an accountancy firm. Three resolutions were passed, as set out below:

"That it is desirable to reconstruct the Company and accordingly that it be wound up voluntarily, and that Francis William Ewart Morgan, of Capel House, New Broad Street, in the City of London, Incorporated Accountant, be hereby appointed Liquidator for the purpose of such winding up."

"That the said Liquidator be hereby authorised to consent to the registration of two new companies, to be named W.J. and M.Mash Limited and H.J. Mash Limited."

"That the two draft agreements submitted to this meeting and respectively expressed to be made between this Company and the Liquidator of the one part and W.J & M.Mash Limited of the other part, and between this Company and the Liquidator of the one part and H.J. Mash of the other part to be hereby approved, and that the Liquidator be hereby authorised to enter into the two respective agreements with such two new companies in the terms of the said drafts, and to carry the same into effect, with such (if any) modifications as he may think fit."

By summer 1936 the split was made official and the two firms began trading separately. On July 28th it was agreed that Mash & Austin would be wound up by September of that year, and a new company formed. In early 1937 HJ 2nd agreed to sell his share of Mash & Austin (which, according to the legal document, "a large part of the wholesale business is in respect of the provisioning of ships and is designated by the parties hereto as 'the shipping business'") to John Martin Mash, the 26-year-old son of Martin Mash, and William Percy Murrell, with WJP and Martin Mash acting as guarantors. An article printed in 'The Chief Steward and Ship Stores' Gazette' in March 1937 had this to say about the purchase:

"An important announcement regarding Mash & Austin, Ltd. We have pleasure in giving as the frontispiece to this issue a portrait of Mr W.P. Murrell. He, with Mr Jack Mash, is managing director of the new firm, Mash&Murrell Ltd, who as of March 31 will take over the shipping branch of the old-established business, Mash & Austin Ltd, founded 67 years ago in Glasshouse Street, off Regent Street, London, by the late Mr H.J. Mash. The secretary of the new company is Mr Martin Mash, who has managed Mash & Austin's shipping department since its inception. The whole of the staff and transport fleet is being transferred to the new company which has acquired commodious

Mash & Murrell letterhead

premises in Henrietta Street, Covent Garden. When the late Mr H.J. Mash opened his premises in Glasshouse Street, his staff consisted of two lads, but he was able to count upon the able help of his wife, a lady of outstanding character and business ability.

"Mash & Austin's initial experience in supplying ships was gained in 1890, when they first began to supply the Castle Mail Packets Company, later to form with the Union Line, the Union-Castle Steamship Company Ltd. An association, not going back so far, but also still maintained, is with the Cunard Steam-Ship Company, for shortly after the Cunard Line began regularly to use the Port of London, the firm were given their first order. Messrs. Mash and Murrell will, we are sure, be able to rely upon the continued patronage of their shipping friends, most of whom, no doubt, know that the firm have in the Home Counties - at Chesham, Bucks,- their own model vegetable and fruit farms."

Mash & Austin continued for some time, supplying the hotel and restaurant trade, but the focus now swung to WJ&M. Mash and Mash&Murrell, both having strong interests in the farms around Chesham and district. Mash&Murrell successfully took on the shipping side of Mash & Austin, keeping current clients and attracting important new ones. In 1939, Mash & Murrell supplied fruit and vegetables to the Canadian Pacific liner Empress of Australia, which was carrying King George VI and Queen Elizabeth to Canada. In subsequent years the firm dealt with many cruise liner firms in the ports of Liverpool, London and Southampton, though as we'll see in later chapters the containerisation of goods and the end of the great days of cruising would put paid to this successful business.

In the space of a few short years the division of the Mash family firm, the virtual demise of Mash & Austin and the creation of Mash&Murrell were, arguably, enough upheavals for any

Will Mash, a keen shot

Bramley Mash

Bramley Mash RIP

business. But there was to be another shock. William James Porter Mash, the rotund, jolly shooting fanatic, popular local employer and mainstay of Torrington Farm, took seriously ill in 1938 and died that same year. He had lived the good life; by all accounts he was fond of a drink and was a very heavy smoker. He enjoyed gambling, horse racing and most sports, particularly cricket and tennis. It is thought he died of cancer and at 56 he was still a relatively young man. In 1910 he had married Nellie Richmond (the sister of my grandmother Lilian Richmond, who was married to Martin Mash) and had three children; Muriel (1912), Alexander (1915) and William (1920). In May 1937 Alexander, who was more commonly known as Bramley (his middle name) died of cancer aged just 22. This must have had a huge impact on the family, and particularly WJP, who possibly saw his first-born son as a natural successor to the business. Whether Bramley's death hastened WJP's own demise we shall probably never know, but it must have had some bearing upon it.

I have a copy of the Bucks Examiner newspaper from May 21st 1937 which gives details of Bramley's funeral. His coffin was placed on a flower-decorated farm wagon pulled by two horses and driven to the church at Ashley Green. Employees of the Mash family, and family members themselves, walked behind the wagon, and pallbearers included members of the loyal Foskett, Dell and Talmer families.

There was a eulogy in the paper which read:

"There is a sadness of farewell in taking leave of one so young and promising as Bramley Mash, and that little corner of the quiet God's acre of Ashley Green where all that was mortal of him was laid to rest will long hold memory in fee. Bramley was not demonstrative, but he was good and thorough, and very pleasant in his manner. He was getting into the business nicely, and whenever you met him on the sports field and quizzed him about being a man of leisure his good-humoured reply as to the hours he had put in that day before he could be free for sport showed that he was careful and thorough. Cricket was not his only sport, but the many who met him on the green field knew that he had a deep love for that game: he was of considerable assistance to the Chesham Club in many ways and served on the committee. Genial, friendly, without side, he was nice to deal with, and a very well-liked colleague. We all hoped that that serious time he had would see him through his internal trouble and fit him to face the busy life he was called for, and his apparent recovery strengthened those hopes but alas it was not to be, and he returned to hospital and did not survive this second serious affair. Alas that it was so: sorrow that we shall see this lad no more, deep sympathy with Mr and Mrs WJ Mash who have lost a good son. Nevertheless Bramley is at rest, safe from pain and stress, and while we sorrow we remember this bright kindly lad with deep respect."

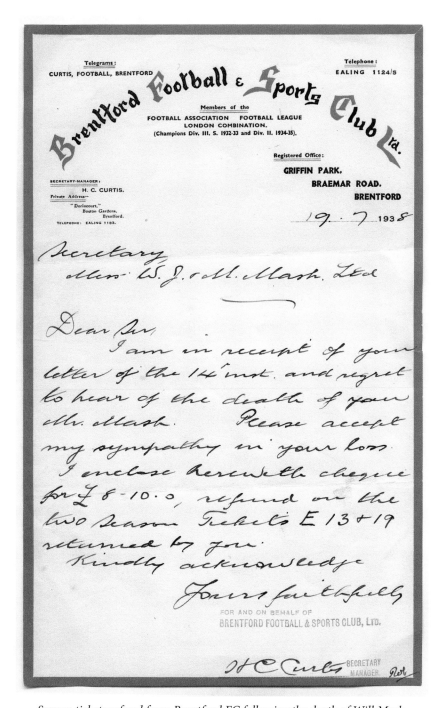

Season tickets refund from Brentford FC following the death of Will Mash

WJP's estate was valued at just over £50,000 - around £3 million in today's money. As Nellie, his wife, was still living she inherited the bulk of the estate, although there was a considerable legacy for his daughter, Muriel, and smaller amounts for friends, relatives and those who had worked loyally for him, including his farm foremen, his secretary, and chauffeur, along with a small gift to Chesham Cricket Club. After his death, a couple of letters arrived which give some insight into his sporting interests. The first was from Brentford Football Club, expressing their sympathy at WJP's loss and enclosing a cheque for £8.10.0 to cover the refund on two season tickets to the club. The second was from bookmakers Ladbroke&Co. Ltd. acknowledging that a cheque made to WJP for £3.15.0 (presumably a win on the horses!) was never cashed and enclosing a new cheque made payable to the Executors of his will. Such gentlemanly behaviour in those days!

These tragedies, particularly WJP's death, would have a big impact on the make-up of the Chesham end of the Mash business. My grandfather Martin Mash, who ran the London office, made the decision to take over at Torrington Farm. His son, John Martin (otherwise known as Jack) would take over his father's work in London and continue with his own firm, Mash&Murrell. Bill Mash, WJP's youngest son would later help my father to run Torrington and the other farms. According to Susan Bayley, my cousin and WJP's granddaughter, Bill Mash resented this. He was only 18 at the time of his father's death and had high hopes of being a butcher. The deaths of his father and brother put paid to his dream and reluctantly he took up work on the farm. He married Ivy in 1942 and died in 1999, his butchering ambitions never having been realised.

I mentioned loyal employees who worked for WJP, and these included Alfred Dell, who was farm manager at Moors Farm, Whelpley Hill, for many years. Alfred lost two brothers in World War One, an unimaginable tragedy that still lingers on in the memory of his son, Don Dell, now 89 at the time of writing. Don - and his deceased brother, Den - followed in his father's footsteps, working on the Mash farms around Chesham for over 50 years. Don lives in the last of the Mash firm's tied cottages - which were provided for all farm managers - close to Moors Farm, where he was based.

"I've lived down here all my life," he told me recently, "and as far as I know I was born at Moors Farm. As a child, I remember hanging off the back of the farm carts as they went to and from the fields. I also remember them fattening up cattle for winter, and there was even a shepherd here then. A lot of pig breeding went on down on the farm.

"I was always around my dad on the farm as a child, and I came to work here properly when I came out of the army after the Second World War. I did a lot of tractor work, drilling, haymaking, baling, everything really. It was hard to start with but as the years went on and you got machinery it was easier. When I first started there were still a lot of horses here.

"Some winters were very cold, nothing like it is today. We don't see much frost now. Worst I remember was the one in 1963, that was a bad one. I was cutting cabbages with a shovel. They were frozen solid. The snow lay from Christmas to March. Summers were warm. I remember 1976, it was a very hot summer. There was a lot of people working on the farm when I was here, most of them were women."

Albert Redding, aged 86, lives in nearby Bovingdon and he worked on the farm as a child, often helping his mother, Kate Redding. He still has a precious photograph of his mother, with farm boss Jack Richmond, foreman Jackie Taylor and a co-worker called Mrs Anderton.

"I was turfed out of school at 13," he said, "and I helped my mother pick peas and potatoes in the fields. The picture was taken around 1935, I'd have thought. These would have been fruit trees in the background. I'm pretty sure it was taken at Whelpley Hill Farm because there was a little orchard there.

"I've a good memory, and I remember a lot of the characters who worked on the Mash farms. There was Mrs Taylor, the wife of Jackie Taylor. Every Sunday morning I walked to Whelpley Hill

From left to right – Mrs Anderton, Jackie Taylor, Jack Richmond,
Kate Redding – drilling seeds, circa 1935

Planting vegetable plants, circa 1935, Jackie Taylor at the back

Farm to take a shilling or maybe two bob or half a crown from my mother to Mrs Taylor, because she ran what was known as a 'diddle'um' club. All the workers gave her a shilling or a penny, whatever they could afford, and come Christmas they got their money all paid back so they could afford Christmas. The term 'diddle 'um' sounds very suspect but Mrs Taylor wouldn't diddle anyone, she was so honest and upright.

"Then there was Whistler Jones. He was a little bit happy go lucky and not quite all upstairs. I used to work with his brother and he told me that two policemen once came to their door, they knocked and Whistler answered and they asked for Jimmy Jones. So Whistler said, 'He's not here, he's up the garden.' Then he shouts up the garden, 'Jimmy! There's two postmen here to see you!' Whistler used to bike from Whelpley to the Bell and Bull on a Saturday lunchtime and found it very hard to ride back afterwards!

"I remember Poppa Clark, who used to follow the thrashing machine around. He bit puppy dogs' tails off for a pound in the days when dog's tails were always docked, and he lived in a pigsty behind the Bull for the majority of his life. He was a local character, and so was Chatty Sears, who looked after the shire horses at Whelpley Hill. Chatty would get them ready to plough, and he was so small he could walk under the horse's belly. When he came to putting the collar on he used to stand on a fruit box. Then he'd put the collar on, and pulled the horse's head down, and the horse would obey.

"He'd plough all day and he'd climb on the gate, sit side saddle on the horse and the horse would walk home on its own. When he got back to the stable he took off the harness and the horse would drink at the trough, then he put the hay and oats in the feeding trough and the horse would do what he said. They understood him, but you couldn't have a conversation with him personally, he was an 'ee arr' man! He used to stick two fag papers together because he rolled his own cigarettes and he smoked Black Beauty tobacco. He lit one end and it was still in his mouth at 4pm, as it kept going out.

"Another thing was pea picking. There was probably 20 women in a field, picking peas all day and there was no such a thing as a portable toilet in those days, they'd just squat down if they needed a pee! I was dragged up there as an eight year old to help my mother. The peas were picked in a round basket called a skip, then they went into a sack, you wrote your name on a bit of paper and put it on the top, then they were weighed and they'd add up the weight on the papers and at the end of the week you'd get paid.

"Win Chalk was the champion, she went down a row of peas, and there'd be masses at first but when it came to the second picking there'd be nothing left. So whoever came next wouldn't get much money. It was hard work, you're bending down all day picking peas. You'd help your mum but after a bit you'd get disinterested and not bother. It'd become a game. It was summer time then, early summer. And it was warm, not like it is today, you could more or less guarantee good weather. They'd do about six hours a day, it was hard work. But we were all fit; my old mum lived til she was 93. Maybe work kept them alive, it certainly wasn't diet because you didn't have a diet. Everyone ate cheap veg and offal, and that sort of food. You'd eat chitlins (pig intestines) and sheep's heads! It's good stuff really.

"The plough would turn up the potatoes and spread them out, then Mr Richmond used to measure out the field and that was your domain, so you rooted about until you found the potatoes. The harrow used to turn the loose potatoes up and you'd wander around collecting them. This was the stage before it was mechanised. It was all done with horses.

"Kids today have never lived. You measure their unriched lives compared to ours. They're all on devices. It's sad. I don't agree with computers and that rubbish. It's not a childhood. They've never climbed a tree, or been bird-nesting or scrumping. We used to scrump Mash apples! We used to pick the rotten apples up in the orchards and they went for cider. Mr Richmond got a bit humpty with us one day so we made a grave of rotten apples, got two sticks and put a cross on it. And he went mad!. You've never seen a man so mad. It was part of your growing up. We did get paid for picking up apples, about 6d an hour. When we picked potatoes we worked our guts out all day for three bob. And your mum took two bob and you were left with a shilling. Do you know, I remember all these things as if it was two years ago?'

Great memories from both Don and Albert of long-gone days, when times could be tough but summers were long and communities stuck together and helped each other - even if they did know everyone's business!

Bill Humphreys, Arthur Hart and Sid Bellamy out fruit picking on the farm

Sid Bellamy and Arthur Hart maintaining the farm's greenhouses

Chapter 6

Torrington at War

By the end of the 1930s, the cloudless days of seemingly endless summers were being swiftly replaced by the coming thunderstorms of war. Even if Prime Minister Chamberlain promised 'peace for our time' following the Munich meeting with Adolf Hitler in September 1938, the rest of the country knew differently.

Despite this, it appeared that nothing much was going to change, at least on the land. Life went on seemingly as before and although farmers (including my late neighbour, Tony Harman) wanted to increase production to help get the country on a war footing there seemed no urgency or encouragement from the Ministry of Agriculture.

That was all to change after Hitler invaded Poland in 1939 and war was declared. Local and county War Agricultural Committees were set up ('War Ags' for short) and suddenly there was impetus to do something about feeding Britain's people at a time when memories of German submarine blockades of merchant shipping during World War One were still sharp.

For Torrington and its satellite farms, the emphasis was on growing as quickly and efficiently as possible to supply food for civilians and military personnel. Many of the great liners became troop ships, and so business carried on as usual with them.

At home, one of the effects of the war in its early days was the influx of Londoners leaving their homes in fear of air-raids. Many of these were children, of course, and in their numbers were children from Jewish schools in the East End, who had more than one reason to fear Hitler's looming presence. This sudden population growth put pressure on small towns like Chesham, not least on school places. In 1938, an educationalist called Christina Adlington opened a school on the corner of Station Road, Chesham, in response to the closing down of another small educational establishment, the Dame School. Chesham Preparatory School opened with just eight pupils, soon rising to 20, and life there ticked along nicely until the outbreak of war.

Mrs Adlington swiftly realised that her premises would never hold the numbers of new children who needed a school place. Luckily, she knew my grandfather, Martin Mash, and he offered her the tenancy of Orchard Leigh House. This site, you'll remember, was purchased as 'Wooden Babylon' when the Mashes first came to the area and bought Torrington Farm. As we know the house later became a health farm and was the forerunner of the famous Champneys spa. By 1940, however, that business had moved to Hertfordshire and the house was considered an ideal place both by Mrs Adlington and my grandfather in which to start a school.

Ernest and Christina Adlington, founders of Chesham Prep School

Mary Adlington, Christina's daughter was in the same class as me at Chesham Preparatory School. She takes up the story:

"When Mum leased the house from Martin Mash the war was on and she already had had two children of her own by then. By all accounts we had lots of evacuees here, as well as Jewish families who had escaped occupied Europe. The house was chock-a-block, with only one lavatory, and there were Jewish families in every room, to the point where mum and dad were almost ostracised because some of the families were German speakers. It was crowded, but that didn't matter if you'd escaped the Nazis or were trying to get away from the fear of London being bombed. Dad had stories of cars just driving up with a mattress tied to the top and the people inside would say, 'Please can we come in'?

"My mum came from a financially poor background, but they were strong Methodists. Dad came from a Nottinghamshire mining family and Dad's father went down the mines aged 13. He came out of the mines at 39 but whilst he was a miner he taught himself Latin, Greek and Hebrew and became a Methodist minister.

"My parents were both socially aware. He was a youth club leader and they met in London. Mum was very intelligent, gaining scholarship after scholarship and eventually went to university. She was very driven on the subject of academic qualifications and she drummed that into her four children, David, Stephen, Mark and myself."

The extended Adlington family, all of whom lived at one point in Orchard Leigh. ①Stephen Adlington ②John Martin, cousin* ③Mark Adlington ④Mary Adlington ⑤David Adlington* ⑥Ruth Randall, foster daughter. (*as seen in class photo of 1940 overleaf)

In June 1940 Martin Mash leased Orchard Leigh House to Mrs Adlington at a quarterly rent of £28.11.6 for three years. At the end of the lease, in 1943, my grandfather sold the school to Mrs Adlington for £2,437 - just over £100,000 in today's money. Mrs Adlington described this as 'great generosity' and it meant they were able to expand the school, extending into a former stable block and creating new buildings.

"I went to the school until I was 10," Mary says, "then I went off to senior school. Chesham Prep was, and still is, a very successful school and has a wonderful caring atmosphere. But like any family business it makes demands on family life, we all had to help. It's the same as if your parents have a shop, farm or pub, the whole family has to pull together to help out. My parents were extremely busy. We sometimes had foster children, relatives, or school caretakers living with us, so the house was always full, like one big extended family. Life could be a bit chaotic, but Mum and Dad were full of love and you could feel that in the house.

Original school building

Class photo, 1940.(① David Adlington ② John Martin)

"My eldest brother David, went to work on Mash's farm when he was 17. He remembers horse hoeing, cattle work and all the myriad other jobs that needed doing. He left to go into the army, but returned for a while after he was demobbed. The rest of us, Stephen, Mark and myself, all worked at the farm occasionally whether it was for holiday jobs, or just filling in sometimes. My son, Tom, worked for Douglas on numerous occasions, especially at harvest time. My parents were great friends with Martin Mash, and Dick and Janet Mash so the connection between our two families has lasted for over three generations."

The Mash Sports Hall, built in 2007

Thursday, July 12, 2007   BUE

News

Headteacher James Marjoribanks with pupils Daniel Khan, five, and Isla Soutter, six, and the children's great grandmother Janet Mash and grandfather Douglas Mash.
Picture by John Blandford C3078-3

Sports hall keeps up family link

by Martyn Pritchard

martynpritchard@trinitysouth.co.uk

A SPORTS hall at Chesham Preparatory School was renamed this weekend after landowner and farmer Douglas Mash.

The Mash family, who have been landowners in and around Chesham for many generations, have been stalwart supporters of the school since it moved to Orchard Leigh during 1946.

Now, following the unveiling of a commemorative plaque, The Mash Sports Hall is set to serve the sporting progress of generations of future pupils at the school.

The unveiling ceremony, also attended by head teacher James Marjoribanks and chairman of governors John Axon, served as a curtain-raiser for the school's annual prizegiving and parents' day.

"The Mash family have been great supporters over many years," explained school secretary Wendy Farrington.

Former pupils at the school include actor and comedian Stephen Fry, who once lived in Chesham.

Some evacuees were closer to home, in terms of the Mash family. My mother's cousin, Jane Lloyd, was sent up to Chesham from Canterbury in 1940 at the age of eight, as the Battle of Britain raged in the skies above her home.

"I came to stay at Woodside with Mr and Mrs Martin Mash," she says. "I hadn't been very well and because I got on well with Janet, their daughter, it was suggested I'd be safer in Buckinghamshire than in Kent. I was made very welcome and although they were strict I felt at home immediately. They were both religious, particularly Mrs Mash, and I was taken regularly to St Mary's church in Chesham, even though I was Methodist. Sometimes I sat by their bed at night while Mrs Mash read the Bible aloud to Mr Mash. He'd lie there with his eyes shut but occasionally he'd open them and wink at me, as though I was in on a big secret!

"I do remember those times so well. I would go to look at the pigs in the piggery but not if they were having babies - children then weren't supposed to see anything like that! The orchards attached to Woodside were laden with fruit, as I recall. I remember standing on the balcony of the house, looking out, and being told that the red sky I could see in the distance was London on fire. It was the Blitz, of course.

"When the Mashes took me to church I never went back to the Methodists. I became a firm Anglican after that and have remained so ever since. They were very correct; everything had to be just so. We had breakfast, lunch and tea and I had to be in bed by the time the gong rang for supper at 7pm. I went to Ashley Green school for a while and I got a lift from the postman in his van if I was lucky!

"Janet and Dick, Douglas and Rosemary's parents, were engaged at that time. I think they met at Jack Mash's wedding. Janet was a bridesmaid because she was a relative of Mabel. We all

Dick Mash, 1940s

thought Dick was gorgeous! He was very good looking and was such fun. I can remember when I was at Woodside Mrs Mash had her sister, Elizabeth, staying there plus her mother, Granny Richmond, who was about 90. They were joined by Aunt Hester and Aunt Agatha, two of Granny's sisters. Dick used to tease Granny Richmond, she laughed and thought it was lovely.

"I was there for about a year, perhaps less, until a family came up from Southampton, which had been badly hit in the Blitz, and there just wasn't any more room. They didn't want me to go, particularly, but I had relations on my mother's side in Ilkley, West Yorkshire, and so I was sent up there. My mother and sister stayed in Canterbury for the whole of the war. My father had been in the First World War and volunteered for the Second, even though he was 40 by then. He was put in charge of requisitioning in east and west Kent, looking at big properties that the army had taken over and valuing the land.

"After Ilkley I went back to Canterbury via some time spent in Sale, near Manchester, which wasn't particularly safe but another relative of my mother's lived there and it was needs must. In 1942 I arrived home and settled into life back in Canterbury. Janet and Dick were married in 1942 and I was bridesmaid. That was a lovely event. Two daughters of Jack Mash were the other bridesmaids and I recall that one was sick during the day and missed the official photographs. I think the excitement got to her!

"Later on I saw Janet often and went to stay with them regularly. My sister came to help out when Douglas was born and we were always very close cousins. Janet used to say that because she was an only child, we were her family - particularly when she felt a little swamped with Mashes! That said, she was a fiercely loyal supporter of the Mash family and its farms."

One of the biggest issues for us as a family business during the war years was the requisitioning of land for government use or support of the war effort. Farmers and landowners right across the UK woke up to find civil servants inspecting their fields and fine houses, and deciding that in times of war, better use could be made of them. Grand country houses were turned into barracks for troops departing to the continent and beyond, while farms saw strange, ugly defensive fortifications built in every corner of their fields.

Under the Agriculture (Miscellaneous War Provisions) Acts of 1940 and 1941 the government were legally entitled to take what they saw fit and in total some 14.5 million acres of land were requisitioned between 1939 and 1945. The Mash farms didn't escape this; one hundred acres of land we owned at Whelpley Hill were requisitioned in 1940 and that winter contractors from

Bovingdon Airfield from the air

The Bovingdon Air Base

John Laing and Son Ltd moved in to build what would eventually become Bovingdon Airfield.

Two runways were constructed, both around 1,500 yards long, and the initial plan was that RAF Bomber Command would use it as a training station before crews moved to the Bomber stations in Lincolnshire and along the east coast. However, world events fairly quickly overtook the Air Ministry's plan. By the end of 1941 the Americans were in the war and the following year Bovingdon Airfield was turned over to the United States Army Air Force, and their iconic B-17 Flying Fortress aircraft.

The first American planes touched down in Bovingdon in August 1942 as part of the Eighth Air Force, the daylight bombing group that, with RAF Bomber Command, took the air war to Germany with devastating effect. With the Americans came all the flash and ritzy glamour associated with the era; visitors to Bovingdon included Bob Hope, Bing Crosby, Clark Gable and Glenn Miller. The crew of the famous B-17 *Memphis Belle* spent time there, and General

Bob Hope at Bovingdon

B17 Flying Fortress

Eisenhower's personal B-17 was housed at the airfield. A very informative and interesting account of the war years at Bovingdon Airfield (and other bases close by) can be found in *'Hertfordshire and Bedfordshire Airfield in the Second World War'*, by Graham Smith. Suffice to say that Chesham and district would never be quite the same again!

Albert Redding, whom we met in the last chapter, remembers the arrival of the Americans very well. As he worked alongside his mother picking potatoes he saw the runways being built, and later had many encounters with US servicemen who indulged mischievous boys like Albert.

"I remember the Flying Fortresses, and the first one landing here. We thought, 'Christ what big aeroplanes!' They were huge. We wondered how a thing like that could fly, but they never let us near the planes to see inside.

"Mr Richards, the farm manager, once sacked a whole load of us boys for throwing potatoes at Flying Fortresses when they were landing," he recalls. "It was at Whelpley Hill Field and as they came in we threw all these spuds at them! But someone in the control tower spotted us and turfed us off the site. Mr Richards gave us the sack immediately he found out, but as we were needed to pick the spuds it didn't last long.

"The Americans coming was the best thing that ever happened to Bovingdon. There was a Mr Rowse, who had a paper shop up the road. We'd come out of school, and go there and collect a whole load of newspapers. We went up to the airfield and sold these to the Yanks. We'd shout things like, 'Two babies found dead in a milk churn!' or 'Hitler swims the channel!' or 'Roosevelt leaves the White House!' All this daft stuff, and they used to buy the papers like no-one's

American servicemen at Bovingdon

business. Two bob, half a crown, whatever we wanted to charge. They'd no idea what half a crown was. Then you'd give the newsagent a few bob and we'd go off with the rest.

"One time me and a couple of other yobbos were sitting by a pond, which was known as Bovingdon Docks, and eating whelks. This American MP (Military Policeman) called Ossie came over and said, 'What are you goddamn eating? You're eating goddamn snails! Are you that hungry? You shouldn't be eating snails, that's all wrong!' So when the next two Yanks came out of the base, he said, 'Look here guys, here's some money, get up the PX and buy these kids some cookies and goodies and fruit.' And these Yanks come back with two bags full of food because they thought we were living off snails. What a day we had!

"The Yanks were alright, though there could be trouble sometimes between them and the locals. In the Wheatsheaf the village blokes would fight the Americans. Someone would say something and there'd be a punch up. I remember one American in the village, drunk he was, and I was down the bottom of the road. He was standing around, firing off his .45 into the air. My father and mother came out, and this bloke's standing by the bus stop with his gun by his side. My dad said, 'Just keep walking and don't look at him. He's drunk over the moon.' Most of them had a .45 but they usually kept it holstered. And he's bang bang bang!'

Bovingdon – The Bell pub then and now

It seems that as well as the Wheatsheaf (which is now a private house) the Americans also frequented The Bell pub (still in business, and owned and run by a good friend of mine, Tim Ward) because, according to Albert, it gained a reputation as a place where the virtue of the local ladies was - to put it politely - easier than in other places!

"I remember the landlord and landlady, Mr and Mrs Pulleyn," he said. "I ran errands for Mrs Pulleyn and she gave me a slice of watermelon. Then, that was something else. Maybe she got it from the Americans. The Yanks used to play card games and we sat under the table and if money fell off the table we picked it up. We never saw so much money in all our lives. One time they were playing and one American standing behind the players was mouthing to his mate about his opponent's cards. The other man found out and pulled out a six inch blade, and threatened him. I was never so scared in all my life. He said, "I'll cut your @#*'#* tongue out!"

As a boy, Des Reid (now aged 90) wandered the lanes around Lye Green and Ashley Green with his friends. "I knew the Mash family," he said, "and they were always so kind to us kids. If William Mash came down and saw us children in the road he'd say, 'You go and play in those fields, in case a vehicle comes down. And help yourselves to raspberries!' But you'd only see three vehicles a day then!"

Not everyone was so generous. Des and his friends (including Tazor Foskett, who would go on to work at the Mash farms for many years) were chased out of Lye Green Farm by one of the workers, Frank Talmer. As Des tells it: "We were climbing trees and when you're younger you don't realise that a bloke who's worked hard all week might be having a Sunday afternoon nap. We were all shouting and making noise, and Frank Talmer came out and shouted as us to clear off. Tazor shouted, 'Oh, alright then you miserable old so and so' which really got this fella's back up, and he came running down the garden path. Tazor was a strong lad, and he reckoned we could escape by jumping from tree to tree! Well, we couldn't and so we started running.

"He chased us though the farm and eventually we ran into a hayloft and climbed to the top of it, hoping he wouldn't find us. When we thought the coast was clear we saw a few open windows and decided to jump out of them and escape. Most of us went through one window but Bill Dell chose a different one. When we landed there was no sign of Bill, so we shouted for him. 'Here!' he said, and you could only see up to his waist - he'd landed in a great big pile of manure!"

During the war Des, then a teenager, drove buses for the Rover bus company around the Bovingdon area, picking up American servicemen and taking them to and from the base. "We started that contract in '43," he said, "and I used to do it 12 hours a day. I drove from the motorpool all through the air base, then up to the officers' mess near Bovingdon Green and turn around there. I'd pick them up and drop them off anywhere they wanted to go. They didn't have to pay, as it was a contract with the Ministry.

"Some of these Americans got killed while they were on raids. The bodies were brought back to Bovingdon and we had to take the coffins to Brookwood cemetery. After the war the Americans requested that they were dug up and shipped back to America.

"Then I got called up for the army so I went in the army and when I came back on leave my uncle (Jesse Dell, owner of the Rover bus company) knew I was around and he said, 'You couldn't do that contract for us?' So I did, and the Yanks couldn't understand where I'd got the suntan from! I said, 'I've just come back from the Middle East.

"I nearly ended up in America myself. I met a female pilot and we got friendly. She was very nice, always wore a short skirt and proper nylons. She asked me to come back to the States with her and I said, 'Oh, I dunno...' So I asked my mum and she said, 'There's no way you're going over there!'

"I remember Kate Redding, Albert Redding's mother. We all used to go to The Bell at Bovingdon and I remember being there one Christmas and it had got to midnight. We'd all had a bit to drink and we were outside, underneath Mrs Humphrey's window. She lived next door. Someone said, 'She'll be in bed, let's wake her up,' so we threw stones at her window. Eventually the window opened and she leaned out. 'What do you want!?' she shouted. Kate said, 'You ought to be in the pub,' and Mrs Humphrey grabbed her chamber pot and said, 'If you lot don't clear off I'll pour this pot on your heads!'"

Days (and nights) of excitement aside, life on the Mash farms was busy. The orchard-spraying records for 1943-1945 show a crew of workers (including the usual contingent of Dells, Fosketts and Puddephatts) working hard across all the Mash farms to keep a steady supply of fruit growing in time for harvest. Looking at the names of the apples and plums being sprayed is like reading an elegy to lost British fruit: Czars, Monarchs, Early Rivers, Pershores, Dwarfs.... Then again, who spends time these days carefully baking an apple or a plum pie? Because of supermarkets and cheap imports we've lost that connection between land and food and while there are a few brave souls championing and growing so-called 'heritage' British produce I fear the genie is long out of the bottle, and cheaper imports rule the shelves.

As Albert Redding mentioned, our farms provided employment for both local young and old, as well as 'out-of-towners'. I know that the Harmans in nearby Grove Farm used German prisoners-of-war to help with various jobs around their farm, but I'm not sure we ever did. It's possible, but I don't have any evidence to confirm or deny it. What I do know is that we had assistance from the Women's Land Army (better known as 'Land Girls') all through the war

Diary of spraying operations, 1943

because one of these was Josie Puddephatt, who still lives locally and is a mine of information about the farms and the local area in the mid to late 1940s.

I spoke at length to Josie during the research for this book and, at 88, still has a brilliant memory for days gone by. She left her home town of Derby at the age of 16 and, just a few months before the war ended, found herself in Cornwall on an 'agricultural holiday' organised by the government. Having worked in a surgical stockings factory from the age of 14, she hadn't travelled much in her life, but far from being homesick, she loved the outdoor life.

"The land always draws me and on the TV it's all country programmes that I watch," she told me. "It's something in me I suppose. Derby was an industrial town, but I'd always belonged to the Youth Hostelling Association and the Girls Friendly Society, and the Youth Club, so I was used to mixing with people and I don't think it leaves you.

Land army girls Margaret, Josie and Cath

"I went on holiday with another girl I worked with in Derby. We went to Porth Leven in Cornwall, and stayed in a hostel for two weeks. We did all sorts of things on farms in the area, and we laughed and danced in the evenings. I thought, 'I like this life'. While I was away VJ Day (Victory in Japan) happened and the war was over. But the soldiers didn't come back straight away, of course, so we were still needed and when I came home to Derby I said to my mum, 'When I'm 17 I'm joining the Land Army', and that's just what I did. It was 1946, and I remember that because it was the year Derby County won the FA Cup!

"I was sent to Great Missenden and put in a hostel, which was a big private house, with 20 other girls. I made two really good friends; Cath, from Rotherham, and Margaret, from Mill Hill. We worked on different farms in the first few months doing all sorts of things. My first day was bunching radishes! After about four months we were issued to Mash's farm and we never left.

"We did everything to do with the crops. We sowed the potatoes by hand, picked them by hand, and we did the hoeing and helped in the barns and the sheds where you'd sort the root crops, the carrots and that. They supplied all the big ships, and once a week they went to Boscombe to a big place that distributed to the shops.

"There was only one tractor there and that was operated by Stick Stevens. He was an old boy, and we had fun with him. Otherwise it was horses; there were about five of them working, then it changed and more tractors came in, big Massey Fergusons.

"Sticks was a little rough fella, he was the father of nine children and we used to rib him like mad, and he ribbed us. He was rugged; proper rugged and scruffy and he kept his tea in a bottle, like a lot of them. I was the littlest one of the three of us and I got teased for that, but I gave it back. I liked Sticks - we didn't get a lot to eat back then, because rationing was still on, and he'd come in the mess house and he give me a lovely bit of his cake. He died with cancer, bless him.

Land army girls Margaret and Josie with Mr Dell

"I always worked at Moors farm. They had everything there; carrots, leeks, peas, spinach - that was a job to pick sometimes. Fruit trees as well. We would have a fire in the winter, and when we had a break at 10am we used to toast a bit of bread on the old fire. Every morning Wyn Chalk toasted her sandwich and the cheese always fell out. We had a lot of fun there. Mr Mash used to get his hair off sometimes, he was alright to us, but he was one to tell us off. Bill (WJP Mash's son, who took over when his father died) wasn't like that, he was jovial. Mr Mash sacked us one day, we were picking peas and we'd had to go over the rows for a third time, well none of us liked to so we all went down the packing shed and we had a go about it, and he said, 'You're sacked the lot of you!' Old Joyce Foskett looked flabbergasted because we'd all got the sack and Mrs Florrie said, 'I can't have the sack'. Then she started crying, but we all laughed and went to work the next day and it was all alright.

"We were picking on piece work. We had a green net bag each and when we filled it we got four shillings. In fact my wedding ring is in one of the Mash fields, a place called Soldier's Bottom. Ron (Josie's late husband) pulled up in the lorry after dinner and he was going to Harrow and he shouted, 'Do you want to come for a ride to Harrow?' I got in the lorry and I was going down the road and I said, 'I don't have my ring.' And it's probably still there somewhere!"

CHAPTER 7

Brighter Days Ahead

The end of the Second World War wasn't quite the end of that story. Britain and its population had changed immeasurably in six years of conflict. The old certainties of the past were gone; instead, the country had to find a way to re-build its shattered economy and come to terms with the loss of its empire. Winning the peace would be as complicated as winning the war.

In post-war Britain, agriculture - like every other industry - had to adapt quickly to new thinking. The 1947 Agriculture Act finally guaranteed farmers fair prices and accessible markets for their produce and, as a result, production increased hugely. And not before time; one effect of the war was that importation of food had reduced significantly and as many of us remember, the rationing which began in 1940 continued until 1954, almost ten years after the war had ended. That said, research and development into all sorts of areas, including agriculture, was speeded up as a result of pressure applied during the war and many of these innovations - including new types of plant, machinery, fertilisers, weed killers, etc - would turn out to be most useful for the post-1945 farmer. Finally, the era of the horse was over.

There was also the issue of the returning demobbed troops hoping to pick up their old jobs on the land. Some farmers simply turned off the Land Girls who had worked so diligently for them during the war years and that, combined with the exodus of former prisoners-of-war, many of whom had laboured on British farms, to their native countries meant jobs were plentiful in those early post-war years.

However, getting rid of good workers wasn't the Mash way. Women like Josie Puddephatt were most welcome at our farms and in fact, Josie stayed on after she was demobbed from the Land Army, working for us even after her children were born. Josie's Land Girl friends Margaret and Cath married local men who worked for the Mash farms, as did Josie.

"I got married in 1948," she said. "It was in the May, just a month after I'd left the Land Army. I got married in Derby and Ron's parents paid for a Rover bus to bring a few guests. I met Ron on the farm. He worked in the packing shed where they loaded the lorries. Us girls did work there sometimes. After we had children we worked down there in the winter with the children in the prams. Old Billy Mash, the other boss who was always joking, once took my Richard out of his pram when he was about 18 months old. And I went mad, because there were tractors, lorries loading stuff, farm machinery everywhere. Not the place for a toddler!

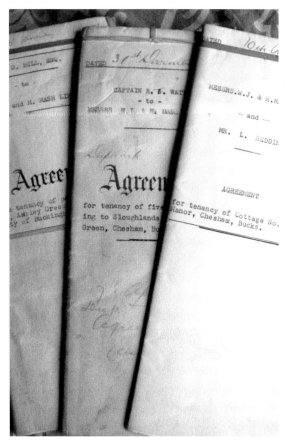

Farm tenancy agreements

"Ron was also a driver and he went to the docks a lot. I remember once his lorry setting on fire at the top of Gore Hill. That was the end of that day's delivery for him! Although his real name was Ronald everyone called him 'Nicky' except for me. And his brother was nicknamed 'Tommy', but he was really called Don. I don't know why they got these nicknames, but they just stuck.

"I remember a couple of very cold winters just after the war. Working outdoors then was hard work all right. They used to drop off a load of dung in the field and your job was to spread it. One winter we went out there and it was all frozen, so we dug out the top to get to the middle which was all right, and I pulled a muscle in my back.

"Sometimes we worked in the piggery and they used to bring slosh and mush from canteens to feed them. When it came it was all hot and steaming and the pigs loved it. They'd eat anything. When you went in the afternoon to give them the second lot, you'd find all these forks and knives and spoons that had been accidentally dropped into the slosh and they were as clean as a whistle. They used to put the cutlery in a sack and sell it on. One day we were in the piggery and one pig had chewed the door and it had its head fast. We had to get a man to come and help. The poor old thing was squealing like mad!"

One of the men returning from conflict to take his place on the farm was my father, Richmond Mash, who was known to everyone as 'Dick'. The name 'Richmond' was, of course, taken from my grandmother's maiden name. My father was born in 1919 and in 1942 he married my mother, Janet Matilda Newton. Jack, my father's elder brother, also married a Newton - Mabel Lilian - whose family were in the shoe business in Chesham. The two ladies were cousins, and while my mother lived in Canterbury she too had roots in the Chesham boot-making business.

My father attended Berkhamsted School as a boarder, but was expelled at about the age of 12 when his father demanded that he attended his elder brother Jack's 21st birthday party. The school said 'no' but my grandfather insisted, and so that was the end of father's time there. He then went to boarding school in Cranleigh, Surrey, and when war broke out he was conscripted as a Lance Bombadier into the Leicestershire Yeomanry (aka Prince Albert's Own). The Yeomanry was initially a cavalry regiment and became a field artillery regiment in 1940, fighting in France, North Africa, Persia, Italy and Austria.

Unfortunately, I know little of my father's war record, only that he was in France after D-Day, pushing the Germans back to eventual defeat. I wish I'd asked him more about it but like many men of his generation he didn't have much to say about his wartime experiences and preferred to keep it that way. Instead, he concentrated on learning the farming business from his father so that when the time came he would be able to take over with confidence.

In October 1951, William Percy Murrell - the other half of Mash&Murrell who had successfully run the shipping side of the Mash business - died at the age of 72. He hadn't been well for a while but had insisted on carrying out his duties with the firm until a few days before his death. Mr Murrell's passing was a sad occasion but along with Jack Mash and my grandfather (who was company secretary) he had helped to establish a business that was very solid indeed and, following the end of World War Two, was increasing its activities rapidly. In fact, according

Detachment of Leicestershire Yeomanry, ①*Dick Mash*

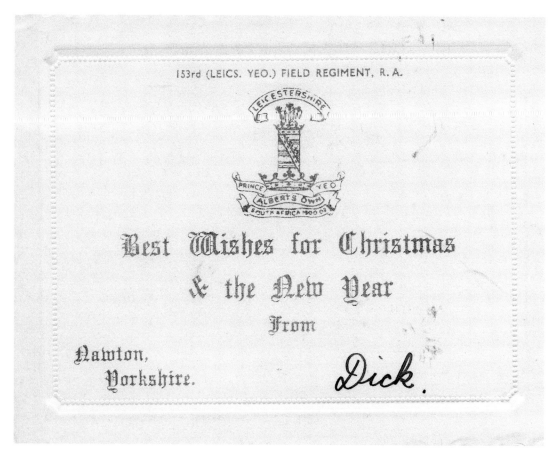

153rd (LEICS. YEO.) FIELD REGIMENT, R.A.

Best Wishes for Christmas
& the New Year
From

Nawton,
Yorkshire.

Dick.

Wartime christmas card from Dick Mash to his wife, Janet on military address card

to *The Chief Steward and Ship Stores' Gazette*, by 1958 Mash & Murrell were trading at seven times their pre-war volume. Now there was no threat to life and limb from U-boats and other enemy vessels, cruising had discovered a new golden age and the renewed fashion for sea travel was led by the Royal Family. In 1954 Queen Elizabeth II and Prince Philip boarded the Savill liner Gothic for their voyage to Australia and New Zealand, and Mash & Murrell supplied all the fruit required for the journey. One of Mash & Murrell's biggest branches was in Liverpool, where many of the great cruise liner firms were based. This was run by John Edward Kimber, who was married to Muriel Mash, the daughter of WJP Mash and Nellie Richmond. John and Muriel were the parents of my family tree-compiling cousin, Susan Bayley. John Kimber was born in Hughenden, near High Wycombe. According to Susan, although he was clever enough to go to university he left without gaining a degree and went to work for the Milk Marketing Board, testing milk on local farms before it was taken away and bottled. This was how he met

Dear Janet,

Please write to me at the address below until further notice.

No., Rank and Name 994121 L/Bdr Mash.

Bn. or Unit 129 Battery

153rd (Leicester Yeo) Field Regt. RA

A.P.O. No. A.P.O. England.

Please tell:— Mother, Father, all at Chesham
(*Here insert names of those to whom you wish your new address to be given*) & Kingshill.

7/43 M45196 12/43 JC&S 702

Wartime letter from Dick Mash to Janet Mash

Muriel Mash and they married in 1940. John Kimber had no ambitions to farm, and didn't want to spend his life within the confines of a farming family, so he eagerly accepted the post of manager of the Liverpool branch of Mash&Murrell.

Although she was born in Berkhamstead, Susan grew up in Liverpool but spent many summers at Torrington Farm in the company of her grandmother, aunts, uncles and cousins, including me! Her memories of the farm in the 1950s and '60s are particularly pleasing for me to listen to, because although Susan and I were born in the same year (1945) I was away at boarding school for much of my childhood and don't have much recollection of day-to-day life at Torrington.

"When we visited Torrington we (Susan, her two brothers and her sister) would be put into a first-class compartment at Liverpool Lime Street station," she told me. "We had sandwiches with us which we had to hide, and when the other passengers got out to go to the dining car we would eat them then. We thought that was a huge joke. Then we'd be picked up by a car in London, and taken to my grandmother's at Torrington House where we would stay for four weeks. She was strict on some things; for example, we'd all have breakfast together then go out around the farm. We had to be back at 12pm for lunch, then we could go out again and had to be back at 6.45pm on the dot for the Archers!

"Grandmother had a lounge and a breakfast room and a big scullery which had a marble counter all the way round. She made her own butter. They didn't have fridges as such, there were cupboards with wire netting to keep the food, and meat was hanging up. There was another room where food was prepared and one which had a huge old fashioned round washing machine, with a mangle nearby. You'd go into yet another room and it was floor to ceiling full of plates and dishes and all the cooking pans and everything. There was also a room where grandmother had all her orchids and flowers, and the tortoises lived there. These had been my mother's, they were called Ben and Tom, and they were over 30 years old.

"We'd come down at Christmas for a big family get-together. The dining room had a Waring and Gillow sideboard and Chippendale chairs. The table featured additional pieces you could slot in to extend it, because there could be at least 20 people for Christmas lunch.

"We had lots of hiding places in that house. One bedroom was full of toys in a cupboard, and you'd go up these stairs, which had been taken out of a theatre, and the bottom was a door, again from a theatre. Apparently grandfather had won it! The stairs split in two; one went to the right where Miss Harris, the housekeeper, had a room. She didn't like children, and we didn't like her, calling her Cruella. If you went to the left the other bedrooms were there, and a huge toilet, with a big pull-chain. The rooms were big with beautiful free-standing furniture, including wardrobes and dressing tables. When grandmother went into a home two ladies from Chesham came and bought the lot for not much money. It all went to America and it was probably worth a fortune but in those days you didn't really know how much furniture was worth.

"I remember us having afternoon tea; there were cucumber sandwiches with no crusts and we all drank out of china cups as we sat underneath portraits of great-grandfather and great-grandmother. When we first arrived we would go out into the orchards and were allowed to eat as many cherries as we liked, which of course we did, and we ate so many it made us so sick that we couldn't face them again. That was the point of the exercise! Later we helped pick them but we wouldn't eat them because we'd got over the excitement of being able to do that. Back in Liverpool I was a bit of a tomboy and so when we visited Torrington I was first up the tree. My sister was four years old and she'd say, 'Susan, you can't do that!'

"Grandmother had two gardeners-cum-handymen who looked after the grounds, which included a tennis court. There was a pig in the garden that we used to tease and grandmother also kept chickens and ducks. One year the fox got in and killed the ducklings and my younger brother got very upset and hated foxes because of it. Across the road, in the farm, there was a piggery and we used to run across the road and with a stick scrape the side of the piggery. Living in Liverpool we never saw farm animals, so it was all a novelty.

"I remember there being a games room partly in the orchard, with a billiards table, and all the workers went in to play. We weren't allowed in so we'd look through the windows. In those days nobody worried about us being out because we'd be somewhere on the farm and the workers knew who we were. They were good times - very different to living in a city. We didn't exactly run wild but we were free to do what we wanted to do within boundaries."

Susan also has memories of the shipping business in Liverpool, and of the city in those days:

"As a child, I remember going on the Queen Mary and Queen Elizabeth with my father in Liverpool. They were incredibly impressive ships. The produce would come from the farms by the lorryload and father would go to market at 4am for whatever the farm couldn't supply. The liner people often complained to my father that items listed on the invoice were missing, and that's because there was so much pilfering going on among the dockers. They seemed to think that taking things was a perk of the job. Containerisation put paid to a lot of that, but it also lost a lot of dockers their jobs too.

Mash staff celebration dinner in packing shed

Pat, Anthony, Susan and Paul Kimber

"We first lived in Ballantrae Road, Allerton, and then we moved across Calderstones Park to Menlove Avenue, which is also where John Lennon grew up. Strawberry Field was near our house. In the house in Menlove Avenue we had a breakfast room with a radiogram and all these records. I used to be in am-dram productions as a teenager so I'd have these people back, listening to music and chatting. We had to keep a room for business people that dad met, and we had season tickets to Liverpool and Everton so we could take business people. As teenagers we went to The Cavern to see the Beatles, just before they became really famous. We also enjoyed watching Cilla Black. It was a filthy smelly place, but the atmosphere was very special. It was a happy childhood both in Liverpool and at Torrington - we were freer then."

Susan eventually married and moved to Bushey, in Hertfordshire with her husband, David, a police officer. She tells me that when they decided to leave Bushey for a new life in Dorset, her grandmother became rather cross and wouldn't speak to her. Susan and David had been visiting the old lady several times a week, and she couldn't understand why they should want to leave the area. Nellie Richmond outlived her husband by more than 40 years and died in 1982 at the age of 95, so she had a good innings by any standards.

The end of the war and a new decade was cause for celebration in various different ways. Every year, W.J.and M. Mash Ltd held an annual staff dinner, usually in March or April, to which all full-time workers were invited. This was regularly held at Darsham Hall, in Chesham's High Street, and was presided over by my grandfather, who was now chairman of the company. In those post-war years of austerity, the menu didn't stray much beyond tomato soup, roast pork and apple sauce and fruit melba, but no doubt everyone had a terrific time, entertained by such acts as Ernie Rutterford's Boys, magician Zicardi, 'singing accordionist' Jessie Speller and comedian Mickey Morris. As we've mentioned, rationing ended in 1954 and the year before saw the present Queen crowned in Westminster Abbey. Street parties and other gatherings went on across the country, and the Mash family didn't let the occasion pass by. On June 2, 1953, Coronation Day, there was a fancy dress parade in Lye Green and when it rained my grandfather allowed the participants to move the festivities to a packing shed on the Mash farm there.

Sandra Dell (now Sandy Carter) who still lives locally, remembers the occasion well. "I was with my best friend Jill Taylor and we were dressed as Hawaiian girls in red, white and blue crepe. Unfortunately when it rained the colours of our dresses started to run! After the party there was tea at the Black Cat in Lye Green and we were all given a Coronation mug as a souvenir."

Sandy is the daughter of Jesse Dell, who started the local bus company, Rover, (mentioned in the last chapter) in the late 1920s. He bought his first bus from the previous owner, a Mr Dunham, who ran buses from Hemel Hempstead to Chesham via Bovingdon. As Des Reid said, during the war Mr Dell had a permanent bus station at Bovingdon Airfield which was used to run bomber crews to their quarters and back. Jesse Dell was a close associate of the Mash family, and would also operate a service to and from Chesham Prep School when the school came to Orchard Leigh House, rented to and later sold to the school by the Mash family.

Sandy is also my age and we found out recently that we were born just days apart in Shardeloes, a country house near Amersham which had been requisitioned during the war for evacuated pregnant women. Around 3,000 children were born there during the war years (including the lyricist Sir Tim Rice, in 1944) so Sandy and I must have been screaming together on the same ward!

"They were great days around here," she told me. "Jill Taylor and I would very often wave down Fred Dell, one of the Mash's tractor drivers, and persuade him to give us a lift on his trailer. 'You two will get me in trouble!' he'd say.

"I remember lots of the local characters around here then. There was Fred Foskett, who worked on the Mash farms and wore a big Stetson hat. He used to wear his best Stetson for his weekly visit to the cinema on a Sunday. Then there was Miss Bangay, from the church at Tylers

The Black Cat pub at Lye Green

Jesse Dell's Rover bus garage at Lye Green

Hill. She used to give magic lantern shows, and at Easter time would put the slides on that showed religious pictures of Jesus .We were fascinated and it was only a glass slide!

"I remember a local lad, Dicky Miles, who spent hours and hours at the airfield. In fact, he spent so long there talking to the airmen that it's said he figured out how to start up a plane, which he did and taxied it around the airfield! I don't know if this is true or not, but it's a good story."

As well as being born in the same place at the same time, Sandy and I have discovered another connection between her family and mine. When HJ Mash died in 1919 he left a comprehensive Will that we have already discussed in this book. Among other bequests, he left two cottages; the first was Lea Cottage in Cookham Dean, left to HJ's 'faithful servant' William Pheby, while the other was Diamond Lodge in Bourne End, to another 'faithful servant' by the name of Daisy Pheby. Of the latter, he says: "I wish to express how deeply I have always appreciated her kindness and sympathy which she has never failed to show me in all my illnesses and troubles for so many years, and I hope my family will always show her the greatest respect."

Quite a tribute, and at the bottom of the will there is a name - Lilian Sarah Anne Pheby, housekeeper at Winter Hill Farm. This, it turns out, is Sandra Dell's aunt, the sister of Jesse Dell and a relation of Des Reid. I'm not sure whether 'Daisy' is Mrs Pheby's nickname, or whether she's the daughter of both servants. Whatever the case, it just shows that it's a small world - and in the years after the war, as we've seen, the world around the Mash farmland was a cosy, insular and close-knit one that would change rapidly as the years went by.

Patrons of the Black Cat, Lye Green behind the pub in the Mash family's fields

CHAPTER 8

Schooldays

To pedal back a little, the end of the war in 1945 was also the year I was born. As I've mentioned, I came into the world at Shardeloes and spent the first six years of my life with my parents at a house called Rosemead.

The war years had a big influence on everyone who lived through it, not least my parents and grandparents. Father was a very conservative man and very careful with his money and while there was some investment in plant and machinery on the farm in the early 1950s, the years following saw few changes.

However, I do remember the story of Ray Milsom, a young machinery rep who arrived at the farm in his green MG soft top some time during the late 1950s. In one session he sold father six tractors, two trailers and a combine harvester, which must have been cause for some celebrations at Ray's company that night! Father reckoned that the considerable outlay required came from the sale of a crop of carrots that were harvested early and covered in straw. The forthcoming winter was very hard and a lot of the carrots growing in the Fens and elsewhere were unable to be harvested, so Father made a killing on them.

"Over the years we did a great deal of business," remembers Ray, "and became firm friends. I spent many an afternoon playing snooker with Dick, and always enjoyed attending many of their splendidly-run functions. On the four farms there were then more than 30 staff to cope with the cleaning and packing of all the fruit and vegetables which were sent up to London daily. One very pleasant memory for me was the blossom and scent of all the Bramley trees in their orchards.

"Douglas was about 24 when I first met him at Torrington Farm. He had just finished his education at Stowe School and was a bit on the wild side, but had a sound knowledge of farming."

Like many other families across the UK at that time, austerity was practiced religiously within the Mash family, particularly in the home. The order of the day was 'make do and mend' and grandmother always knitted a dozen pairs of socks every year for all the male Mashes. Everything else was either darned or sewn back together. When you consider that rationing didn't end until 1954, almost ten years after the war finished, you realise what damage the conflict had inflicted on Britain's economy.

Even as a small boy I knew I wanted to work on the land. They had a job to keep me away from the farms and buildings in the early days. I loved being there and one of my earliest

Doug Mash, aged 5

memories is watching the men collecting the hay. Back then they didn't bale it; it was all collected up into ricks. When the hay was made into silage it was put into concrete tubs and molasses was poured on top of it to make it smell sweeter. In the winter you'd cut the silage out with a fork and it was rather ripe by then, leaving a lingering smell on your clothes. In the yard there was a drain and I once fell into it. It was two feet deep - quite a splash for a small boy - and I was covered in slurry, making me unpopular for a while. I remember seeing all the cows chained up and milked by hand. Then the overhead lines were put in so that they could be milked automatically. The milk was then conveyed to the dairy where it was cooled and I recall seeing it flowing into the refrigeration process and then put into churns. These were lifted on to a ramp and Chesham Dairies used to collect them every day.

Den Dell operating an early-model combine harvester

87

I used to watch the threshing machine in action and I would ride the tractor with Don Dell as the sheaves of corn were collected. As we've said, Don was the son of Alf Dell, the foreman at Moors Farm, and he had a brother called Den. Den was a terrific ploughman and both brothers were very loyal to the company for many years. There was also Tazor Foskett, whom we met in the last chapter as a young boy. He was one of the company lorry drivers and again, fiercely loyal to the Mashes. He was known as the 'godfather' of the company and he made it pretty clear that he expected everyone to do what he wanted them to do. If you were loading his lorry with vegetables it had to be done in a particular way, otherwise he would get quite agitated - to put it mildly!

One thing the family didn't skimp on, however, was education. I was at Chesham Prep School - still housed in the former Mash property of Orchard Lea - for six years until I was sent away to the Old Ride School at Little Horwood, Buckinghamshire, about 30 miles from Chesham. Looking back, six or seven seems very young indeed to be sent away to school, but that was what happened among well-off middle-class families and so it was taken for granted. Inevitably, perhaps, my memories of those days aren't always pleasant. Every morning started with a cold bath followed by a run (in nothing more than pumps and shorts) to the bottom of the school drive and back, which was about a mile. A large-built matron made sure you stayed in the cold bath and each day the time you spent increased by several seconds until by the end of term it felt like an eternity. It was meant to toughen you up, as were the beatings regularly dished out for the most minor of offences. I remember being given six of the best by the headmaster with his cane for talking in dormitory - I was seven years old at the time. The only thing I enjoyed was sport, which I was quite good at. Otherwise, it was a regime of casual brutality and I hated it. We used to come home for a weekend every four weeks or so, and either Father and Mother or one of the firm's lorry drivers would pick me up and drive me back to the farm.

We were encouraged to write letters home each week and, being well brought-up little schoolboys we did not tell the truth about the bad times in school. My mother kept some of these letters, particularly from Coronation year, 1953, so I would have been about seven or eight at the time. A selection of them are below:

The Old Ride,
Little Horwood
9.5.53

Dear Mummy and Daddy,

I like my school more every day. I can read your letter without help. We are doing different kinds of sums every day, adding, taking away, multiplying and dividing and also £.s.d. sums. We start doing easy ones and then they gradually get harder.
Thank you for my bat and gloves - they arrived safely.

Love,

Douglas.

The Old Ride,
Little Horwood

Dear Mummy and Daddy,

I hope you are quite well. I have finished my cake and it was very nice. I would love The Eagle comic if you can get it. We are not allowed to have any other comic here. We did not play cricket yesterday because it rained a lot. I have had two pluses this week. I have made 14 runs this week and was not out. I am in the top division at school in Form I.
Some men are thatching the roof at school.

Lots of love,

Douglas.

The Old Ride
Little Horwood
27. 6. 53.

Dear Mummy and Daddy,
                    I am looking
forward to seeing you on Sports-
day. I hope I can win a race.
I hope your little chickens are
quite well. We have got a
jackdaw in the school and the
boys take him on their shoulders
and in the morning when we
have breakfast he comes in and
makes us laugh. We have
got a table race chart and
all the boys in our class
have an aeroplane in it. We
have to fly round the world

Letter from Doug Mash to his parents, 1953

The Old Ride,
Little Horwood
6.6.53

Dear Mummy and Daddy,

I am enjoying myself very much. Thank you very much for taking me to London to
see the decorations yesterday. Please would you send my cake. Thank you for the cars.
I hope you caught Jenny Wren alright. I hope Granny and Grampi are quite well. I am
looking forward to seeing you at the weekend. Please could we go out to dinner in
Aylesbury and have a picnic tea. Mrs Watt caught some newts in the goldfish pond
and we brought them indoors. In the night they jumped onto a rock in the middle of
the basin and escaped. I expect they returned to the pond.
Sorry, we have just found one of the newts dead on the floor.

Lots of love,
From Douglas.

Following Old Ride I was sent to Stowe School, also in Buckinghamshire. The school is one
of England's most famous public schools, not least because of the outstanding late 17th century
colonnaded mansion which forms the core of the school, and gardens designed by William Kent
and Capability Brown. The whole place was beautifully laid out but again, I didn't enjoy the
regime of 'fagging' (where younger boys acted as servants to older pupils) or the regular beatings.
However, I did like the opportunities for sport at Stowe and I really enjoyed cricket, rugby and
hockey.

I can't claim to have excelled academically at Stowe. I did enough to get through but that
was it, and I much preferred the sports field to the classroom. The days were long; unlike prep
school we only ever came home at the end of half and whole terms, so there wasn't much time
spent at home during those years. When I did arrive back at the farm I would get stuck into
whatever jobs I could assist with. I missed the outdoor life and working with men like Don,
Den and Tazor. At Christmas I used to help dress the poultry with Stan and George, two of the
farmhands also assigned to this task which involved plucking the dead birds and removing their
intestines. In the early days I was nowhere near strong enough to kill them, but I remember
Don and Den killing the bigger stags (male turkeys) by putting their heads on the ground and

Stowe School, 1950s

laying a wooden bar across their necks to break them.

I also spent a lot of time riding in the lorries, taking produce to the big ships docked in the ports of London and Southampton, or working with the tractors. No-one seemed particularly worried that I was a young lad, albeit that I was tall for my age. Health and safety was practically non-existent then; the belts on the threshing machines were all exposed and if you got your hand trapped in there you would lose your arm, or worse. Even so, farming was the only thing I wanted to do. I didn't think much about the time when I'd eventually take over; I was just interested in general aspects of farming really. I used to enjoy loading the lorries until 8pm at night, lifting boxes of plums. I used to bag up all the cauliflowers up and weigh them, and the peas.

By this time Father and his cousin Bill (WJP Mash's son) were running the farm. They had separate roles, with Bill looking after the spraying and the fruit while Father was more involved with cereals, cultivation, seeds and the cattle. I remember Bill trimming cauliflowers alongside Tom Taylor, a farmhand. Once Bill had taken the leaves off he'd throw the cauliflowers to Tom to pack, and as he did so Bill would call out the three sizes - 'dozens, 18s and 24s' - so they could be packed into the correct crate according to size. Father dealt with the beef and dairy herds, and was very keen on his Hampshire Downs sheep. The reason they had the sheep was because they fitted in well with the root crops. They could be folded in with the crops and once the vegetables were eaten, off went the sheep to market. The sheep were lambed in a little field along the Lye Green Road and I remember that it was always a wonderful highlight of the agricultural year to see the lambs jumping on bales of straw. When the lambs were fat enough, at about six months old, they'd go to Tring market.

My grandfather, Martin Mash, was still involved at this stage. He had terrible arthritis (possibly the result of spending so much time outdoors) and had trouble walking. However, he had a chauffeur called McLeod, who used to bring Grandfather to the packing shed and he sat in his wheelchair, wrapping apples all day long. All the apples for the ships had to be individually wrapped with the WJ&M Mash logo on the paper. Then they were all put into cardboard boxes that had the Mash apple logo on the side, with 'London, Liverpool, Southampton and Chesham' underneath. Grandfather loved doing this job; it kept him occupied and busy and got him out of the house. In addition, he still attended business meetings with 'the boys'. He died in 1967 and some years before he passed away he made a significant decision to transfer his shares and property to his two sons. Unlike previous generations he had only two children which made any decisions about family inheritances so much less complicated, thereby avoiding family conflict.

William Hockey, chauffeur to Martin & WJP Mash

The eldest boy, Jack, had the London business in Covent Garden and a half share of the London property. The reason it was a half share is that the other half belonged to Will Mash, who had died in 1938 and which resulted in my father running the farm with Bill. In return Jack and Dick (my father) had to provide him the income to support the lifestyle he wanted. I do know those decisions were the right ones and thanks to the trust the boys would carry out his wishes, enabling grandfather to lead a good lifestyle and be cared for in his own home, Woodside, right to the end.

Retaining a chauffeur was part of the 'deal' struck when Grandfather handed his portion of the farm over to my father. He'd always had one, even when he was able-bodied, and just recently I met up with Roger Hockey, whose father William ('Bill') Hockey was the driver both to Martin and WJP Mash. Roger gave me some interesting details about his father and the time he spent with the Mash firm:

"Dad was born in 1910 in Dolphin Square, London. His father was killed on the Somme and in 1924 the family moved to Southend. Just after that, Dad's mother re-married, to a South African, and we know that Dad stayed in Southend until about 1934. We then lose him for a year or two but I've a feeling that he came to the Chesham area then because he married my mother, Ethel Dell, whose relations worked for the Mashes. She was related to the Dells at Lye Green. Her mother was Rhoda and she was the sister of Alf Dell, at Moors Farm.

"I'm pretty sure my father worked for WJP Mash as a chauffeur up to the point that he died, then he worked for Martin Mash. I have an elder brother whose name is Albert William Bramley, and I think he was named Bramley after WJP Mash's son, who died so young.

"At the start of World War Two dad went into the army, but he was injured early on in the fighting and invalided out. He then came back to continue working for the Mashes and during the war they would let him have days off so he could collect wounded soldiers in an ambulance from Southampton Docks. Quite soon after the war he left the Mash firm and began driving for a woodware factory in Chesham. Some time in the '50s or '60s he was contacted by Bill Mash, who wanted him to drive Muriel Mash (daughter of WJP Mash) around for a few months. I think it was because she'd been ill, so he happily did that.

"Dad loved every second of working for the Mash family. Sometimes he drove a fruit and veg lorry for them but mostly he was chauffeuring family around, including children. He also looked after the cars as best he could unless it was a major job. He was driver, chauffeur and handyman, and evidently there there were quite a lot of cars up here. I sat with my dad at the Mash centenary dinner in 1996 and he said it was the best day of his life, seeing all those people there from his past."

Well, it's quite hard to imagine any farmer having a chauffeur these days!!

Back to the story…. I left Stowe School with six O Levels, which wasn't bad considering I wasn't academic, and it was enough to get me into an agricultural college. First, though, I needed to complete two years' training on a farm before I was eligible for such a college - and that farm couldn't belong to my family. Father had the solution. He was a member of a national committee which advised on fruit-growing and met regularly in London. He was the representative for Buckinghamshire and he sat next to a representative from the Wisbech area of Cambridgeshire. We were still producing fruit then, so Father thought it would be a good idea for me to gain some experience in this area. After conversations with the man from Wisbech it was decided that I would work on a farm belonging to a man called Alan Hudson. So, at the age of 17 I packed my suitcase (not for the first time in my life!) and left my parents in Chesham for a whole new set of adventures in Cambridgeshire.

CHAPTER 9

The Prodigal Son

I hope I'm not dishonouring the memory of my parents when I say that although I loved them, and they loved me, we didn't share a particularly close relationship when I was growing up. As I've said, I was sent away to school from a very young age and so the day-to-day bonds which other children share with their parents were, if not exactly broken, somewhat fractured by my absence from them.

As I entered my teens a feeling that I needed 'parenting' in the more conventional sense nagged at me. Having spent so long at boarding school I was quite an independent character but I did feel something was missing in my upbringing. Fortunately, my sabbatical to the farm in the village of Wisbech St Mary coincided with meeting Ron and Pauline Peters, with whom I lodged up there, and who I consider to be my 'second' mum and dad. They had no children of their own, and they didn't know me from Adam, but when they were asked whether they would take in a callow 17-year-old from Buckinghamshire they said 'Yes'. And so began a close friendship that has lasted more than 50 years, a relationship I truly cherish.

Ron, who died some years ago, was an area manager for a potato supplier, and had been asked by the farmer I would be working for whether they'd be able to put me up. They were a close couple, having met during the war in Flamborough, East Yorkshire. Ron was in the Royal Navy and they met at a dance. Pauline, now 93, is Bridlington born and bred but nonetheless she moved down to Cambridgeshire in 1948 to be with the man she'd married.

I arrived almost straight from school, and I was pretty green all round. I never really knew what a social life was until I moved in with Ron and Pauline. So let's allow her to take up the story:

"Douglas came to us in 1962, he was about 17 then. I'd never had anyone lodging with us before but I said 'Yes'. Then he came on the Sunday with his mother, father and grandma, and when we met him we knew we'd made the right decision. He was a lovely lad. We didn't have our own children, but it wasn't from choice. I'd had cancer twice, and was unable to have them, so it was like having a son when he was about, which was lovely for us.

"We watched him growing there, and on the farm, and we had a lot of laughs with him. He hadn't had a drink until he came to the village, so my husband said, 'Well, we'll go for a pint'. We lived next to a pub and when Douglas came back he said, 'Oh, I didn't like that beer, it was horrible stuff'! He's changed since! He was a sociable lad and he quickly made friends with other boys working on the farm, and lads in the village."

Dick & Janet Mash; Janet receiving an honour for work with Medical Comforts in Chesham

It's true - the first pint I ever had I didn't like at all and, having a sweet tooth, I asked for a glass of port instead! The pub regulars must have wondered where I'd landed from, but after a while I learned to appreciate the taste and would often join Ron for a game of snooker at the Working Men's Club in the evenings. I was really enjoying the work on the fruit farm and life was good. We'd spend the winters pruning the trees, and later in the year we'd be picking and packing, loading lorries and shifting fruit to the cold stores. It was mainly apples; cooking apples and dessert apples, plus plums and pears. The farm had a piggery too, and they would spread the manure under the trees for fertiliser. The farm employed a reasonably large

Doug Mash (back) with ① Ron & ② Pauline Peters &, ③ sister Rosemary ④ and father, Wisbech

workforce, some 30 people in total and mostly from Wisbech St Mary, and they were a great gang. We'd all go out dancing in Wisbech on a Friday night, and one of the first live groups I saw was Manfred Mann, who played at the Corn Exchange in 1963. I was being paid around a fiver a week in wages, half of which I gave to Ron and Pauline and the rest was spent on entertainment, which I was growing rather fond of!

"We didn't much mind what time he came in," Pauline says, "but he was never very late, and especially during the week when he had work the next day. We hardly had to tell him off but if we didn't like something we always said, and he'd never take the hump. During the time he was with us his parents bought him a Mini and to have a car was quite the thing, so he had a lot of friends who wanted rides all over the place! I remember that he took some of the local lads down to meet his parents and he wore a black shirt. I said, 'Oh Douglas, that'll never do, your mother won't like that shirt!' He probably wore it anyway. I think that was the time he had an accident in the Mini…"

Indeed it was. We'd visited my parents and decided to have a drive around London. I had a bit of a collision with a Skoda on Hyde Park Corner and Skodas weren't built very well in those days so I imagine he probably came off worse. We weren't injured, just a few bruises if I remember. I was certainly finding my sociable side, anyway, and it was in Wisbech that I met my first girlfriend, a young lady called Pam Richards. She was from a place called Benwick, which at the time was known as the 'dirtiest village in England'. It was a big sugar beet growing area, along with potatoes, and when the beet lorries came out of the fields they were covered in mud which seemed to stick to the roads all year round.

While I enjoyed it, the work on the farm was strenuous and you were very tired when you got in, especially in the winter when you'd spent all day cold and wet. I was always very pleased to return to a warm house which felt like home. It's strange - I remember exactly where I was when I heard that John F.Kennedy had been shot, and that was in Pauline's lounge, just about to have my dinner.

"He wasn't a fussy eater," Pauline remembers, "but he didn't like onions or garlic and he still doesn't to this day. Otherwise he wasn't hard to feed. He liked meat and two or three veg and he loved Yorkshire Puddings, though he found it strange that we ate them first as a kind of starter. That's the traditional Yorkshire way and I think he thought it was a bit odd. Mind you, he soon got used to it. I'd always make him a packed lunch to take to work and cook him a meal for when he got home. I mothered him, I suppose.

"On summer weekends we'd take off for the Norfolk coast and Douglas would always come with us. We'd have a picnic and a game of cricket on the beach at Brancaster or Sheringham."

While I was living with them Pauline had another bout of cancer and I moved out while she recuperated. I went to work on another farm so that I could get a greater variety of experience, and that was mainly arable. We harvested a lot of peas, which went to the Smedley's canning factories across East Anglia. It was a very different business to fruit but I'm glad I saw it because if I'm truthful, the fruit growing was in decline, at least around Buckinghamshire. Father wanted me to see how a fruit farm worked before I took over the Mash business but at this end it was already in decline. Our fruit trees were older and less productive that the ones around Wisbech, and eventually we would grub up all the Mash orchards, so in the long run the experience didn't help me much. The soil in the Fens was far more productive too.

That said, I did some real growing up during the time I spent in Cambridgeshire and I'm forever grateful to Ron and Pauline for putting up with me and being such good 'foster-parents'. They are times I will always look back on with affection and while I always knew I would return to Torrington and manage the farms I'm very pleased I've kept my connections with Ron and

Pauline Peters and Doug Mash, 2015

Pauline. They taught me to be sociable, and to be kind to people, and I shall always be grateful for that. They visited the farm many times, sometimes to see my parents, with whom they'd become friends, and when we've had parties and occasions to celebrate.

My relationship with my father, while not always close, was cordial and as Pauline pointed out when I spoke to her for this book, he always listened and took on board any suggestions I had for the running of the farm. As we'll see in subsequent chapters this wasn't always easy for him, and no doubt there were certain aspects of my management here he definitely didn't agree with, but he let me have my head and I'm pleased about that. One aspect of the farm work that I enjoyed doing with him was around Easter time, when the farm valuation was done. I'd accompany father and the auctioneer around all the farms, looking at all the land, livestock, buildings and machinery. It was a stock-take, if you like, and I always found that very enjoyable, knowing what was here. My mother was also supportive - perhaps not quite in the maternal way I would have liked but nonetheless she was there, and trusted me to make good decisions on behalf of the business. Socially, she was an active person and was very involved with the local St John Ambulance Brigade. For many years she ran the Medical Comforts Depot in Chesham, which hired out wheelchairs and other medical aids to local people. In 1978 she was presented with the insignia of Serving Sister by the St John Ambulance organisation at a ceremony in London.

So I had many happy times in Wisbech and after that I attended Shuttleworth Agricultural College in Bedfordshire. There, I met Peter Morley, an Irishman by birth who had been at school in England from the age of eight and was aiming for a career in farming. Peter and I hit it off straight away and because there was no college-based accommodation on offer during our first year we shared digs nearby with a couple called Mr and Mrs Field. Peter takes up the story:

"Mr Field was a slightly studious sort of man with white hair and glasses, and somewhat deficient in humour, I thought. His wife was a very nice lady, with very red cheeks. Doug and myself used to share a room and when I first arrived there, Doug had a car; a Mini Countryman. He used to drive me from the Fields' house into college every day and I sat beside him in the classroom. He used to keep copious notes, well written and presentable. I, on the other hand, used to lose my concentration and my notes were a bit deficient in many ways, and illegible. Sometimes Doug used to disappear for the day and I'd be left to take the notes. I don't think I supported him very well in his absence!

"When we used to go to college, Doug would spray copious amounts of Old Spice over himself before he went out, so it was quite pleasant to travel in his car beside him. I think it was his way of being; he always had a nice sports jacket on - it was a dark moss colour with light orange squares on it - and he had a pair of twills and a fine pair of stout farming shoes.

"We had a good few adventures. He was especially nice and kind and thoughtful to me, and nothing was too much trouble for him. At the time I wondered why he had this Mini Countryman because it seemed too big for purpose. He would disappear at weekends to March, in the Cambridgeshire countryside, and I knew he liked market gardening so I presumed he was furthering his education in growing carrots or something. Subsequently, I discovered that in fact he had a dual-purpose vehicle. He had a lady friend in March though I didn't ask who she was, because the less you ask the more you hear! But I think he may have been having some fun in the back of that car!

"I saw him at a 50th anniversary reunion there two years ago and it was really lovely to meet up with him. He came to pick me up at Luton Airport and I wondered if I'd recognise him at all. When you come out of the customs area there is a little area of decking and Doug was sitting up there, the same old beak peering around the corner. It was great to recognise him after all that time.

"I recall him being a very keen sportsman. He loved his cricket and was a very solid bat. He also played hockey, which I know nothing about but he tells me he was a good hockey player. I used to say, 'Sure, the only reason you play hockey is that you wouldn't be good enough to play rugger or soccer.' He'd look at me disdainfully and say nothing, which is the best way of dealing with an eejit!

"He used to bring me down to his family's place near Chesham and it was there I met his mother, father and sister. It was a lovely old Tudor house, very interesting architecture, wooden beams. There was a lovely warmth there, not only from inside the house but of the feeling within. His mother was a very nice warm person and quite correct in her ways. His father had a good head of grey hair, a bright eye and a strong moustache. He was very upright and had a good figure for his age. He always had a nice tie, representing a cricket club probably.

"When I finished at Shuttleworth I worked a herd of dairy cattle in Essex for a while before going back to Ireland to work with my father, who had a business in shipping. Eventually I started my own shipping and transport company, but it is one of my regrets in life that I didn't go into agriculture or become a vet. When I saw Doug recently I had a look round his farm and he showed me his prize Limousin cattle, which he's rightly very proud of. And he says to me, "Peter, stand in the middle of the yard, I'm going to let the bull out." He opened the gate and this enormous creature came forwards that must have weighed two tons. I had no stick or anything, but I'd been around livestock to know that I should stand still. So that's what I did, and the bull ambled gently past me. I think Mr Mash was trying to test my nerve!"

After Shuttleworth I went back to the Fens for another year. So by the time I returned home I was heading towards my mid 20s and had discovered a certain degree of freedom; freedom from schools and freedom from parents. The problem was that my parents - particularly my mother - didn't acknowledge that I'd changed. In their eyes I was still a boy on leave from boarding school and was treated that way. I was told what clothes to wear, when to wear them and what time I needed to be in. It was a case of mothering long after it was really needed and, having felt strangled in the school system for many years, decided to rebel. I moved out of my parents' house and into my own property, and immediately felt much happier. I wasn't hugely able to look after myself but I struggled by, buoyed up in part by my membership of the local Young Farmers' club. The fun I had with the local lads and girls on the farms around Wisbech was about to be replicated on my home territory! The aim of Young Farmers is to make sure that young people working on farms aren't isolated, and have the chance to get together, pursue their interests and raise money for various causes. And probably drink a bit too! I became involved in the South-West Herts branch and we had a huge amount of fun organising dances and fund-raising events for local charities.

Pam Richards and Doug Mash (DM's 21st)

One of the most memorable things we did was to drive a tractor from John O'Groats to Land's End. This took place in April 1969 and we hoped to beat the world record of 57 hours for the 876-mile drive. We also decided to tow a lifeboat on a trailer behind a Land Rover to raise money for the Royal National Lifeboat Institution (RNLI). The reason for this was that a month previously, a ship had got into difficulties near the Orkney Islands. The Longhope lifeboat was called out but got caught up in heavy seas and gales, resulting in the deaths of all eight of the crew. Ironically, all the people on board the vessel which had asked for help were saved when the boat eventually ran aground. It was a terrible disaster and we felt that if we were heading to the north of Scotland we should do something for those brave men who had lost their lives.

Jesse Dell, of the aforementioned Rover bus company, lent us the Land Rover and we had an old tractor with over-sized tyres lent to us by George Brown's manager Ray Milsom that we took up to John O'Groats on a Foden beer lorry lent to us by Jack Sunderland. Tazor Foskett, the loyal Mash employee, drove it up there for us and we set off with every hope of beating the record. Well, it was something of a chaotic trip (as you can imagine!) in the days before Sat-Navs and even though we were sleep-deprived we all took turns in driving the tractor and the Land Rover. I remember one lad driving, Jim Saunders, who accidentally took the tractor down the sliproad to the motorway before he was escorted off by the police. Although we didn't break the record we did get to Land's End in a pretty respectable 65 hours and raised £950 for the RNLI. The most generous place we travelled through, I remember, was Wigan!

We also did several 'ploughing marathons' for charity, including one on the Bucks/Herts border at Flaunden. We used seven small red tractors and ploughed up a 150 acre field in 48 hours, setting an unofficial record. We only stopped to re-fuel and have a bite to eat, and in total we were paid 25 shillings an acre for our services. It was very tiring, as I remember, but in the local paper I was quoted as saying that we wanted 'to have another bash at it next year.' Oh, the energy of youth!

We certainly had a lot of fun in the YFC and eventually I rose up the ranks to be chairman of the county. I'm still in touch with some of the people I met back then, and I'm pleased to say they are still rascals!

One of those people from my YF days is Eleri Roberts, who was in the Caernarfonshire Young Farmers Club when I first met her. She's still involved in the organisation and is now County Organiser for Clwyd Young Farmers Club.

"I've known Doug a very long time," she said. "I met him at a YF annual general meeting in Llandudno in 1970. We were in the Caernarfonshire club so we were the locals and we

A ploughing marathon

THE SIGHT of a little red tractor ploughing across a Chiltern hill is commonplace. The sight of seven little red tractors running amock on one farm means that something very odd is happening.

But that was just the case on the Bucks border at Flaunden over the weekend. Seven little red tractors, taking from Friday night to Sunday night ploughing up a total of 150 acres of land, and only stopping briefly for refuelling.

This was South-West Herts Young Farmers' Club, who set up an unofficial record with their non-stop ploughing marathon at Moonshine Farm, Flaunden.

The club, comprising members from Chesham and surrounding areas, were paid 25 shillings per acre for their services.

TIRING

The members took it in shifts to drive the tractors, and stopped briefly to re-fuel the 12-gallon tanks, and a bite to eat. All food was provided by the girl members of the club.

The marathon was to have continued until six o'clock on Sunday. But when the Young Farmers ran out of land to plough, they had to drive to another farm seven miles away, and plough another 20 acres.

In all, the club worked some 46 hours, and that's an awful lot of ploughing. Said member Douglas Mash, of Ashley Green: "It was really tiring, but we want to have another bash next year."

Part of the money earned will go to local old people's charities at Christmas.

Tired and weary after some 46 hours in the saddle, that's tractor-mounted David Fox of Croxley Green, and Douglas Mash, of Orchard Leigh, Chesham, after the ploughing marathon over the weekend. They still managed to raise a smile for our photographer, however

David Fox and Doug Mash, ploughing marathon, early 1970's

NATIONAL FEDERATION OF YOUNG FARMERS CLUBS

Patron: Her Majesty The Queen

Royal Smithfield Show 1970

National Beef Cattle Judging Competition

THIS CERTIFICATE IS AWARDED TO

Douglas Mash

Hertfordshire

FOR HAVING REACHED THE STANDARD
AS SET BY THE JUDGES

President

Doug and friends at a party, Western Australia. ①*Eleri Roberts*

decided to provide entertainment for our guests from across the country. There was a group of girls, including me, who sang and played guitars so we sang at the AGM and Doug came up afterwards and chatted to us.

"He was there with a crowd of Young Farmers from Hertfordshire and we all hit it off, so much so that some time later a load of us - three cars full - went down from North Wales to Hertfordshire as their guests. We sang at a barbecue they were having and Doug and his friends found us all places to stay and we had a great time. I remember that Doug had an MGB car with a cowhorn attached to the front of it - a typical young farmer!

"Doug was a very sociable person who would talk to anyone and that's how he got in with our lot. We all spoke Welsh and he was quite fascinated with that. We've kept in touch ever since and seen each other in different places. I was in Australia for his 70th birthday, and last year he invited us down to the farm and took us all to Ascot. We've kept up a good friendship over the years.

"I'm still working with the Young Farmers organisation. Without agriculture where would this country be? It's important to look after farmers and farms, large or small. Young Farmers got up to pretty much then what they do now. Which is having fun, raising money, having a dance and a drink and socialising. They work hard and they play hard, and that's how it's always been!"

CHAPTER 10

The Young Farmer Knuckles Down... Mostly!

The Young Farmers' side of my life was fun, yet it was something of a safety valve for most of us involved, because in the late 60s and early 70s making a living on the land was changing rapidly and if you didn't keep up you quickly went under.

The post-war boom in British goods was coming to a close as global markets expanded and produce could be imported and exported much more rapidly by air. The days of the great cruise liners calling in at Liverpool, Southampton or London were in decline as passengers found it much easier to fly to sunny destinations and board their boat there, rather than trudge to British ports and set off on a three-week voyage to the Caribbean.

The increase in containerisation was also having an effect on growers like the Mashes. Whereas once only carts, then lorries, took produce to markets, the advent of the standard container meant it could be transported by sea and rail. The bags and boxes that took so long to pack and unpack were made redundant by the container, which speeded up the process and needed far less manual labour than before.

There was also changing consumer tastes. The speed with which goods from abroad could be shipped, packed and delivered had increased dramatically and suddenly former 'luxury' items were within the range of the ordinary shopper. The supermarkets that were beginning to replace the old-fashioned local grocery stores spotted this and began to pile produce high and sell it cheap. The days when housewives devoted whole mornings to baking apple or plum pies were numbered; 'home-made' was replaced by 'ready-made' as we entered the era of convenience, and it was often no longer so convenient to buy local. Whoever was first to market ran off with the prize.

All this had an effect on farmers across the UK, who had to cut their margins and, in many cases, lose loyal workers. Josie Puddephatt, the former Land Girl who stayed on with us after the war was over, recalls that by the late 1960s she had left farm labouring behind, and gone on to work in a factory. And who could blame her, when factory wages were on average around £10 a week more than you might earn on the land? We were one of a dwindling band of agricultural employers who still offered tenanted cottages to full-time employees, even after their retirement, but even that wasn't always enough to attract good workers.

A lot of the above thoughts were swirling around my mind as I settled down to work with Father and Bill at Torrington Farm and I knew that, someday at least, I would have to make some very hard decisions as the man in charge. For the moment, though, life carried on much as it had done, albeit with a few nods to the modern age. Chemical fertilisers were being updated all the time and we had various chemical company representatives visiting us with a view to selling us their products. One of these was Ian Gillott, who is now retired, and was more successful than most when it came to selling father and Bill his wares. He takes up the story:

"I was a science teacher in Lincolnshire, which is where I married my wife, and I got a Head of Department in Amersham. The move nearly killed us financially, so eventually I applied for a technical representative's job with Murphy Chemicals and had an interview in the Crown in Amersham. The reason I got the job was that I was a reasonable cricketer and the sales manager was fanatic about cricket!

"This would be about 1968. I had to do some training, then after two or three months I went out on the road with an experienced rep, Bill Bryant, who Bill Mash adored. He had been a navigator in the war before going on to university. He was very well liked; he looked like Father Christmas, didn't take life too seriously and was a wonderful teacher. He would go to the biggest fruit grower in Oxfordshire and say, 'I've managed to get you a couple of tons of captan' (a fungicide) and there would be no debate over price.

"Then Bill retired, he was a keen sailor and he moved to Lymington. Before he went he said, 'I want to take you to an old friend, Mr Mash at Chesham.' He introduced me to Bill, who always seemed to be by the apple grading machine. They were supplying most of the liners back then. We had a conversation mainly about Brentford Football Club, what was wrong with it and how he could put it right!

"Bill Bryant, Bill Mash and I walked the orchards and from that moment I pretty much left Murphy and set up two distributorships for them, which was unusual in those days because most companies dealt directly with the farmers. One of the distributorships offered me a new car and more money to work for them directly, so I did. I moved to Wokingham but I continued to see Bill Mash. He could never remember my surname so I said, 'It's Gillott - like the razor blade.' One day I went into the office and someone said, 'there's a chap been ringing for you but he seems to think you're called Ian Wilkinson!'

"Bill was a great guy to work with. He'd listen very carefully to any advice you gave him, but he wouldn't always take it. His orchards were a bit untidy - today you'd probably call them 'natural' - but he knew about balance and if I suggested that we combine a weedkiller and a plant protector he'd claim the balance would be upset. I thought he was a Luddite back then, but today he'd have been on the button.

"What he did accept was good control of pests and disease, and I would suggest ways of doing this, with which he agreed. The main pests of apples were aphids and caterpillars, and

Bill's standard programme was to use two chemicals; one was DDT and the other BHC, both of which would horrify people these days but back then they were standard sprays. Bill's main problem was the apple scab fungus which begins with a black mark on the leaf and goes on to the apple. I would write a programme out for him and that would usually be mycocide, which was captan mixed with mercury. Then a new 'wonder fungicide' came out called Captafol and we were told it was much safer than using the mercury compound. But after two months we were told to stop selling it as the drift was bringing people out in a rash. Bill was most disappointed as it was working very well! You wouldn't use any of those chemicals these days, as they're all banned - probably not surprisingly.

"I went to see Bill one day and he wasn't looking happy. He said he'd had lot of trouble with a gun licence and had been to the local police station where he'd dealt with a sergeant. 'And do you know,' he said, 'the man was a Welshman?'! I thought that was very funny. I was very fond of Bill and we got on very well. He had his idiosyncrasies but you don't come across people like that now. It's all business, business, business - there was none of that then.

"Things have changed now, but it was the proximity to the London markets which made the Thames Valley in terms of its growing capabilities. A lot of foreign labour was used even then - mainly Italians and Spaniards. There were grower-salesmen here, people who would grow fruit and vegetables, take it to market and sell it themselves. I found it hard to understand that business model so one day I went down to the old Covent Garden market and saw how it worked, and it gave me new respect for the guys who would get out of bed so early to do that.

"I have very fond memories of Bill and the Mash family, and I have been very fortunate to deal with families like this in the Thames Valley."

I very much enjoyed fostering the kind of relationships the farm had with people like Ian and would seek to make new ones every time I took a lorry full of produce down to Southampton or London. If you had time you might get the chance to go on board the ship, look around a bit and meet the crew, which was fun. I was trying to be like anyone else working on the farm, just learning about the different aspects of the job and seeing how the farming year all fitted together. I don't think I was treated any differently because I was the boss's son and while the workers perhaps didn't quite see me as 'one of them' I did what I was told, enjoyed the work and learned a lot in the bargain.

During the 1970s, an agreement made during the Second World War came to fruition for the Mash family business. The land at Whelpley Hill that was requisitioned by the Air Ministry in 1940 to create a large part of Bovingdon Airfield was, by the early 1970s, considered by the Ministry of Defence to be no longer useful for their purposes and so a clause inserted into the original agreement allowed us to have first refusal to buy it back. We did just that, and bought back around 100 acres, of which 40 acres was concrete and the rest arable land, and we paid reasonable money for the lot. There may have been a temptation to dig up the concrete and turn the whole site back to farmland but if there was, it was no more than a passing thought. As I've said, by the 1970s earning a living from farming was ever more challenging and agricultural businesses had to look at new and innovative ways of using their land.

We saw the potential for the concrete straight away and we began to let some of the old buildings to fledgling businesses (one of the first was a camping and leisure retailers) and other entrepreneurs who thought they could make efficient use of the old airfield. Interestingly, when Bovingdon was still in the hands of the RAF the airfield was used as a location for several war films, including '633 Squadron' (1964) and 'The Battle of Britain' (1969) until all flying stopped there at the end of the '60s. However, in later years it would become popular as a location for more general films, which we will look at further in this story. For now, though, it was good to have back an asset that had been long-lost.

Filming '633 Squadron'

Chantal and Michelle

Personally speaking, events in my life were changing too. One evening in about 1975 I attended a Young Farmers meeting at a club in Kings Langley. It was a country and western theme night, and after a few drinks I plucked up enough courage to ask one of a group of nearby ladies if she would like to dance. Her name was Joan and yes, she did want to dance so off we went. She was a friendly person and we hit it off, although she did let me know she was already married. Some months later I had a knock at my door. There on the step was Joan, who had left her husband and had been working at a hotel in Dunstable. I let her in and, to cut a long story short, we eventually married and had two daughters, Chantal (born in 1977) and Michelle (born 1979).

Sadly, it wasn't a marriage that would last. We just weren't suited, and my schooling and background hadn't given me a great deal in the way of worldliness, particularly around women. However, we did have two lovely daughters so that was something.

Just before I met Joan I decided that I'd take a little time out from the farm and go to visit New Zealand. I guess they'd call it a 'gap year' now, but it certainly wasn't a year - more like a few weeks! I'd heard a lot about the place and I really fancied seeing something of that part of the world before I knuckled down to life as a full-time farm manager. At the time I was playing a lot of hockey (as well as cricket) and one of the guys in my hockey team, Greg Thurston, was from Perth, Western Australia. He suggested that en route to New Zealand I visit and stay with his parents in Perth, so I took him up on the offer.

And so began a 40-odd year love affair with a city and a country that I've come to regard as a second home. I've never been a huge fan of cold, wind and rain (though as a farmer I've had to grit my teeth against it often enough!) and I found Perth's climate to be entirely compatible with my temperament. I loved the people, the landscape, the attitude to life - and I loved watching cricket under guaranteed sunshine. I came back raving about the place and I knew that over the years, farming demands or not, I would be a regular visitor to Australia. Just after Chantal was born we went out to Sydney as a family, staying with Joan's brother Steve. It would be a few more years before I went again but by then I was divorced, and had a vague dream that one day I would make a home there.

I was, and still am, a sociable guy and I found that the natural sociability of the Australians suited me. That's not to say I wasn't sociable when I was back in England! I made many good friends around the area; people that I'm still friendly with today. Tony and Kate Barber are just two such people. I met them both in the early 1970s and we still keep in touch. We met through

Chesham Cricket Club, early 1970s. Fathers and sons match.
① *Jack Mash* ② *Geoff Keen* ③ *Reg Plested* ④ *Dick Mash* ⑤ *Doug Mash* ⑥ *Eddie Greenham*

our mutual love of cricket - Tony and I were playing for Coleshill Cricket Club and Kate helped out with the teas. During the fruit harvesting time I'd ask people from the club to come up and help, and they'd raise money for whatever was needed up there.

"Doug asked me to go apple picking for three weeks," Kate remembers, "and I stayed six months! It was around the first time Doug went to Australia. He used to invite us up apple picking to raise money for the club, so I went with my friend Sue and discovered it was a life I liked. We went picking as a group on a Sunday and the Mashes would make a donation to the cricket club for us doing so. It helped to extend the pavilion and put in new showers and dressing rooms.

"I started working there more often and I even borrowed Doug's car for a while. If you needed it you'd just come to pick it up, and the following day I'd pick up a friend then we'd drive through the lanes in time for work and get home in time for the kids. Tony did his fair share of tractor driving up there too. We did all the different jobs - we didn't mind what it was. I remember once going into the Post Office on the way home and they looked shocked because we were so dirty!

"Doug was well known for his parties at Woodsides when his parents were away. We'd all go out to the local pub and end up back there for a few hours. I remember Tony telling me that he went up there once and Doug showed him a cupboard that was full of Chivas Regal whiskey!

"I remember Tazor Foskett, he was a typical old country gent and used to tease the life out of me. He had to load his lorry himself - he wouldn't let anyone do it for him. Tazor was always fond of Doug.

"Working on the Mash farms was hard work but good work and everyone mucked in to help. There must have been 40 of us there then, and we all got on well. They were good days."

They certainly were, and as the '70s ticked by I continued working for Dad and Bill, trying to shape the ideas I'd have for the farm when I eventually took over. There would be hard decisions to make, but I looked forward to the challenge of making my mark at Torrington and continuing the good name of the Mash family in whatever form.

CHAPTER 11

Apples and Cattle

By the end of the 1970s both Bill and Dick Mash were close to their 60s and ready to hand over to me. I'd been involved in the decision-making for some time up to this point and had had to take one of the biggest decisions ever made in this particular business - that of getting rid of the Mash orchards.

It certainly wasn't an easy thing to contemplate. The business was founded on fruit and vegetables and Mash apples had been served on cruise ships heading to all parts of the globe. Even the company's London headquarters in Glasshouse Street had (and still has) an ornamental pineapple on its roof. To cut away the very thing that had made the Mash name well-known seemed almost a sacrilege.....but times had changed and the economics of growing fruit on the scale we were used to were no longer adding up.

As I've mentioned, containerisation and what we'd now term globalisation were all helping to import perishables, including fruit, that consumers demanded all year round. Apples could be picked in South Africa one day and be on Britain's supermarket shelves the next. Our storage methods couldn't compete with that level of freshness, and consumers were also enjoying discovering new foreign varieties of fruit. The humble Bramley wasn't having much luck against the likes of the exotic Kiwi Fruit! Equally, the competition from more productive growing areas of the UK, such as Lincolnshire, was having an effect and in my mind the only solution would be to free up more of our land for cereals and possibly livestock.

Bill and my father also found this decision difficult. There were many discussions and arguments back and forth, but in the end they too saw the sense in what I was proposing. The trees in question were now around 70 years old and were coming to the end of their useful growing life, commercially speaking. They were quite large, making picking ever more difficult and our full-time labour force wasn't getting any younger. Good workers who had spent much of their lives on the farm tending the trees were, like Father and Bill, contemplating retirement. Don and Den Dell, for example, ended their time with us as part-time gardeners for Father up at Woodsides. Besides, the farm itself was needing less and less employees - the effects of increased mechanisation.

So we started to chop the 200 acres of trees down while slowly reducing the dependence on fruit. For a few years we did good business logging up all the timber and selling it for firewood. Apple wood is particularly good for this as it burns slowly and has a pleasant smell. Getting rid

Banger racing

Bovingdon Market

115

of the orchard took about 15 years in all, as we could only work on it during the winter months when we were less busy with the arable side of the farm. There were a couple of cold winters during the early period and I recall selling around 100 tons of wood each of those winters, making a nice profit for us.

A few activities up at the Bovingdon site were bringing in money too. Various people

Aerial view of Bovingdon airfield in more recent times

approached us to use the site for their businesses, including a haulage contractors, a car rentals company, a firm selling camping equipment and garden furniture and, for a good few years, a company that held banger stock car racing events. In the early 1980s a plan was put forward to build a new prison on land adjacent to our part of the former airfield. This was approved and the contractor was the Wimpey construction company. We agreed that they could deposit all the excavated materials from the construction site for a significant fee, and that afterwards they would landscape the waste into a 'bund' or a mound that would give some environmental screening. After several years' work HM Prison The Mount opened in 1987 and was initially operated as a Young Offenders' Institution. Over the years we've built up the bund and while there has been some controversy around this, mainly involving the local council, we've tried to make that part of the site look as decent as it can.

Over the years there have been various proposals for the airfield's old control tower, which is on our land and close to the prison. It is in a state of some disrepair and in 1995 the council said they recognised that, apart from the runways, the control tower is the last visible remnant of the old airfield. They suggested that while a major development to fund its restoration and include a small museum was an option, it was likely to be very expensive and therefore, for environmental reasons, its demolition was a better way forward.

Bovingdon airfield control tower then and now

Area	Application No	Development
		NOT FOUND ON PLOTTING SHEETS
L	0276/95	Siting of two porta cabins
Unknown	1790/88	Waste transfer station
N	0691/88	Temporary site office
6	1719/87	Access and car parking for open
J	1025/87	Use of land and buildings for m... plant
K	0839/84	Restoration to agriculture, landscaping, formation of bu...
	1256/81	Cat C Prison (outline)
H	0775/81	Lattice mast, building secur...
C	0927/80	Mast (45m), building and
	0593/78	Details of vision plays 4/1095/76
I	0290/78	C.O.U. of agricultural l... (farm shop)
I	0248/78	Vehicular access b...

Area	Application No		Development	Decision	Date
			BOVINGDON AIRFIELD: PLANNING HISTORY		
1	0933/96		Recycling facility for inert material in association with clay extraction operation and refill of void	Ref	25.00.00
	1166/95	CM	Recycling facility for inert material		
	0172/94	CM	Recycling facility (clay extraction)	Gra	22.05.96
	1434/91		Extraction of clay for brickmaking and restoration of worked area with inert soil and spoil	Gra	24.02.95
	0583/89		Disposal of waste materials to raise level of land	Gra	08.12.94
2	1236/87		Earth banking to form shelter belts	Ref	25.07.89
	0373/82		Car park for open air market and access to classified road	Ref	04.12.87
				CP	02.07.82
3	0133/76	CC	Bovingdon Bypass		
4	All Chiltern P/A			No Objection	01.04.76
	1438/80		Showroom and sales office - landscaping details		
	1045/80		Showroom and sales office	Gra	06.10.80
	0279/80		Prefabrication building for showroom	Gra	20.08.80
5	0495/77		Demolition of store and extension of building	Gra	21.02.80
	0940/95		Retention of extended market area and parking	Gra	10.05.77
	0939/95		Operation of Sunday car boot sale	Gra	20.09.95 DN
				Gra	20.00.00

Bovingdon airfield's many planning applications

In the early 2000s I was contacted by James Murphy, a former American air force serviceman who was proposing a rescue plan for the control tower, which would see it turned into a joint RAF-USAF museum. It sounded a good idea but, as the council suggested some years earlier, a lot of money would be needed to bring the building up to scratch and sadly the plan came to nothing. It is sad to see it in such a state but I fear it is now beyond any salvation.

All that said, the runways have seen plenty of use (which is just as well, as the concrete is 20 feet deep in some places and a phenomenal amount of work would be needed to remove it). As well as the banger racing (which stopped in 2008) a very successful Saturday and Bank Holiday market has been held on the site for the best part of 30 years. This is leased from us by Wendy Fair Markets, one of the UK's biggest market operators, and it has proved a very successful venture for all concerned, with more than 400 stalls appearing there each week.

Recent filming in Bovingdon

118

As mentioned, the runway has been used for filming since the 1960s and continues to be used by production companies, mainly American, right up to the present day. Some years ago the government gave film companies certain tax breaks and that, plus the fact that Elstree and Pinewood studios are not far away, has brought in good business for us. The runway has been used for films including The Fury (starring Brad Pitt); Harry Potter and the Deathly Hallows Part One; Rogue One: A Star Wars Story; Sherlock Holmes and Fast and Furious 6, among others.

So the airfield ticks over as a good business for us and it may be that in future years developers might want to build houses on it. If I'm still around we'll have to make a decision about that but for the moment I'm more than happy with the various activities going on up there.

Back to the 1980s and a rule which crept in towards the end of that decade, completely transforming the way we farmed at Torrington. Where we had grown cereals we had always burned the straw that remained once the crop had been harvested. It was a quick and highly efficient way of getting rid of the remnants of the harvest, killing weeds, slugs and other pests, and up until the end of the 1980s most arable farmers followed this practice as a matter of routine. However, by the turn of the decade there was a strong lobby in favour of banning straw-burning, on the grounds that it caused pollution from smoke and had an inherent risk of fires spreading. The government of the day listened and banned stubble-burning, causing a lot of resentment among farmers.

Personally, I always liked to burn straw. You did it straight after the harvest and it was a lovely clean way of killing off weeds. With the wind in the right direction you burned the outer three rows first and quickly it would spread across the field, leaving a very clean black surface. If you did it right you could almost drill the next crop in immediately.

So when the ban came into force we had to decide what to do with all the straw. I pondered, then decided to make an investment in some Hereford Friesian cattle. In the past there had been dairy cattle on the Mash farms but this was before my time (or at least before I was old enough to work with them) and in any case I had no experience with beef cattle. Through trial and error I eventually got to grips with the

Paul Walker with Ronick McAinsi

Ronick Matador

husbandry required of beef cattle and finally the time came when I could put the cows into bull - i.e. allow them to have calves. I sought advice about the best breed of bull for the job and, overwhelmingly, I was told that Limousin cattle made for very easy calving. I followed the advice, which was correct, and I began to form a liking for the Limousin breed.

Limousins come from Limoges, in the Central Massif area between central and south-west France. They are hardy creatures, and healthy ones too; muscular but without excessive fat. They only arrived in Britain in 1971 but by the mid-'80s they had established themselves as the UK's premier beef producing animal. I could see the potential in establishing a herd of Limousins and, encouraged by what I saw, I invested in a few heifers from the Tanhill herd in Devizes, Wiltshire, and gave myself an education in this well-tempered, well-balanced breed.

Following that, I made my way to Carlisle, one of the biggest cattle markets in the UK for the Limousin breed. It was there that I bought Ronick McAinsi, then an 18-month old maiden heifer with an excellent pedigree, for the princely sum of 28,000 guineas (almost £30,000). It was an awful lot of money for one cow but we were doing well back then, not least because of the various activities at Bovingdon airfield, especially the market. Sometimes it pays to invest, even if it seems a big outlay, and I had a feeling that I would be rewarded by McAinsi in time.

Unfortunately, my father saw the situation rather differently. He thought I was stark raving mad for paying out so much money for a single animal and made no bones about saying so. However, he didn't disown me; in the end he had to trust me and he understood that if I got it wrong it would be me with egg on my face.

Luckily, my instinct proved correct and although Father didn't live to see it, the Brockhurst Herd became one of the UK's premier breeders and dealers of Limousin cattle. In 2004 McAinsi won breed champion at the Royal Show in Warwickshire and from her came a winning streak of progeny including Brockhurst Batik (breed champion at the Royal Highland Show, who sold for 22,000 guineas in 2011); Brockhurst Bolshoi, who was inter-breed champion at the 2014 Great Yorkshire Show and breed champion at the Royal Highland Show in the same year;

Domino, Interbreed Champion at the Royal Highland

Brockhurst Howzat (Bolshoi's daughter) who was reserve inter-breed beef and Limousin champion at the Royal County of Berkshire Show in 2014, and Brockhurst Heavenly, who was Supreme Beef Champion at Berkshire Show (2015) and Interbreed Champion and Overall Champion Limousin at Great Yorkshire Show (2016).

Towards the end of the 1990s the closure of the Banbury livestock market in Oxfordshire meant that the only specialist Limousin markets were in Carlisle and Stirling - both a long way from Torrington. To compensate, we decided to build our own on-farm sale ring and in April 1997 we held our first breeders' sale here at Torrington. The sales carried on successfully for some years until we decided to finish them in 2011. Quite a few of the Limousin breeders from the south east had finished what they were doing and the sales were no longer so viable. However, the breeding side of the herd went on unabated and in 2016 Millington Highlight, from a herd near York, sold for an amazing 50,000 guineas. Highlight's mother was Brockhurst Option and her mother was none other than…you guessed it….Ronick McAinsi!

Doug McBeath is a freelance stockman and also farms in Scotland. For a number of years now he has come down to Torrington Farm during the show season, helping us to prepare our Limousins for the big events.

Dougie McBeath and Doug Mash

First sale at the Torrington sale ring

"We first met in 1991, I think it would be," Doug says. "It was through cattle breeding. We have a small herd in Stirling and we met at the Royal Show at Stoneleigh Park in Warwickshire. I think he'd just started into Limousins at the time, and we were Champion at the show that year. Doug later bought a daughter from the cow we were champion with. As a breeder, he stood out! A lot of the other guys keep themselves to themselves but Doug is a real people person and he enjoys nothing more than a drink with the stockmen.

"He's always been very fond of the summer shows and if you go to a show you go to see what the Mash family has brought, because they like winning! I now show his cattle for him; I come down and prepare them for the shows. I used to take the cattle to Scotland but with various restrictions it wasn't working out so well, so now we show down here and I come down when he wants me. We do a sale in October and April and he sells a lot of cattle in Newark. He likes them properly fed and in the right condition, so my department is to make them look as pretty as I can and walk them round the ring.

"I first showed cattle for him in 2008 at the Highland show. We were Champion in 2008, 2012 and 2014, and within that we were Reserve Interbreed with Batik and then Interbreed Champion with Domino, and Supreme Champion with Batik's sister. As for Doug himself, he is without doubt the most generous and honest guy I've ever worked for."

Brockhurst herd victory, East of England Show

A pair of farmers I've had a long association with regarding Limousin cattle are Tom and Rita Evans, who now live in Suffolk but are originally from Cambridgeshire. We met around 30 years ago at a pedigree cattle sale in Banbury, Oxfordshire, and were both starting out in Limousin breeding.

"We had bred commercial cattle before," Tom says, "but I had got fed up with feeding commercial cattle, looking after them and all that, with the end result that they went for meat. I wanted something more out of it than that, so we went to Banbury and bought a couple of cows. They were £5,000 each - that was a shock to the system when commercial cows went for about £400! Anyway, we sold about 24 of our commercials to pay for them and the first calf out made £4,500 the following year so we realised that was the way to go, and we'd made the right decision.

"So later on we bred a well-known bull called Fenrose Drifter; he went into a stud farm, and did very well for us. By that time we had sold quite a few to Doug, including Hattie which he kept until she was 19. He took her to the Royal Welsh and won with her. Our dealings with him led to a good friendship and over the years we've put cattle into the sales at Torrington. That did us very well because it got our names around. Then I bought a bull in partnership with Doug and again, that did us very well. So it was a combination of a very good friendship and a trusted business partnership: we bought from each other, we sold on his farm and we all did well out of it.

At the Herts Show

"When we decided to retire, my three sons couldn't afford to go into the business, so we decided to sell the farm. I was 68 then and my wife kept saying, 'It's time to give up, you silly old sod'! We just did it on our own, me and Rita, calving cows at night and training bulls. Taking cattle to places like Carlisle is hard work, especially when you're getting older, and can be dangerous on your own. So we sold up and Doug was good enough to buy the whole herd in one hit and hopefully he's not regretted it.

"I know he's pleased with them and he says if the cows being loaded into the truck suddenly just stop, he knows they're Fenrose cows! Doug is generous to a fault, he's very sympathetic to everybody and anybody who needs help. He has always been that kind of character and he gets a kick out of helping people. I think that's his lifestyle, he enjoys that. We don't see him as much as we used to but he gets over when he can, and when he does we always go out for a good lunch."

Breeding and showing has kept us busy for many years now and it pleases me to see the Brockhurst Herd thriving into the 21st century. Just down the road from us, our farming neighbours the Harmans have the Chesham Herd of Charolais cattle, another French breed

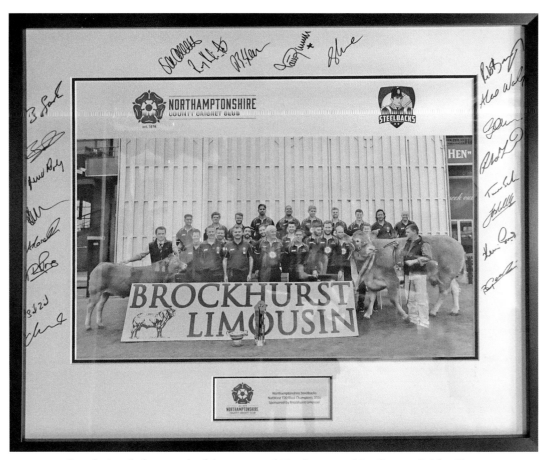

Doug's signed photograph of the sponsored Northamptonshire County Cricket Team

which came to England about fifty years ago, before the Limousins arrived. This herd has been successful and it's quite interesting that two neighbouring farmers got into French cattle and did well from them.

In 2016 I combined my love of cricket and cattle breeding by sponsoring the Northamptonshire county cricket team under the 'Brockhurst Limousin' banner. Success in the show ring was matched by success on the cricket field as the Northants Steelbacks became NatWest T20 Blast Champions that year, beating Durham in a brilliant match that was only settled in the final over of the game. I was so thrilled and proud to be associated with the team's success that day, just as I have been with the past and continuing success of the Brockhurst Herd.

CHAPTER 12

Celebrating Old and New

A s the '80s rolled into the '90s the need for manual labour at Torrington continued to decline, as it had been doing since mechanisation really got underway after the Second World War. When our long-standing employees retired they weren't replaced - but they were looked after in accordance with the principles of the Mash business, which was to provide former employees with accommodation and a pension for the rest of their lives.

In 1991 we celebrated the retirement of five of our most loyal workers, with no less than a combined 250 years working on our land. The five were Den Dell (67), Don Dell (65), Fred Dell (65), Percy Puddiphatt (72) and the legendary Willy 'Tazor' Foskett (74). As mentioned earlier,

Staff picture, King George VI Cup for Best Managed Farm, 1993
①*Mike Riddle* ②*Mark Lake* ③*Brian Redding* ④*Harvey Mash* ⑤*Doug Mash* ⑥*Brian Toft* ⑦*Fred Dell*

Left to right; Tazor Foskett, Den Dell, Percy Puddiphatt, Don Dell and Fred Dell

Don and Den went on to work as part-time gardeners for Father and at the time of writing Don still lives in the farm cottage he has occupied for many years.

The retirement of the 'famous five' marked the end of an era in which successive generations of families worked on farms right across the UK, knowing the land and its business intimately. In our case, no more Dells, Fosketts or Puddiphatts working at Torrington was a strange thing indeed, particularly for me who'd grown up with these men that I'd regarded as mentors and friends. Their loss reduced our workforce to just four people: 50 years previously it had been 140.

However, just as the old English farmhand's way of life was disappearing, a new breed of farm worker was making its way to these shores. On Easter Monday, 1994, while I was working in the farmyard, I was approached by a young man pushing a bicycle. He had a pleasant, open face and a broad smile.

"I'm sorry to bother you," he said, in a strong Eastern European accent, "but I was wondering if you've any work for me? I've been to the farm down the road, they got nothing, but they say maybe you do?"

'Down the road' would be the Harmans' farm. 'Thanks, Tony,' I thought, 'for palming

The five retirees in the barn

Andrejus Simkus

him off to me!' But the guy looked strong, willing and cheerful. I asked him where he'd come from.

"Lithuania," he replied.

"So you've come all the way from Lithuania to find work? On a bike?"

"I take bike on a bus from Warsaw," he said. "I arrive in London, and I get on bike, cycle around, see if there's work."

The man told me his name: Andrejus Simkus. He'd cycled up to Watford, sleeping wherever he could and asking around for work. Somehow he'd arrived in Chesham and had ended up in Grove Lane; first at the Harmans' and finally at the Mashes.

Well, it was coming summer and strong pairs of hands are always useful on farms around this time. So I gave him a couple of jobs….and almost 25 years later Andrejus is still with us and plays an integral part of the working life at Torrington Farm.

I liked him immediately. He was straightforward and honest, and determined to make something of himself in this country. He worked for us for six months then went back to Lithuania and unsuccessfully tried several times to work again in the UK before finally returning for good in 2005, when Lithuania had been admitted to membership of the European Union. In those years he'd been turned back twice at Dover, had joined the Lithuanian Army (having already had a spell in the Red Army as a teenager), lost a lot of money when his bank collapsed and worked in Sweden. Yet he never gave up hope of making a life in England and I admire his determination to create a better life for himself and his family.

"My cousin was in Sweden," Andrejus says, "so he says 'you can come too' and I worked on a golf course for a couple of summers. And then in 2004, when Lithuania joined the EU, I said, 'I need to take the chance and travel to find work'. So I write a letter to Doug and I ask, 'May I come to do work for you, because now it is open borders and you can travel'. And he says, 'Yes you can come'. So I finished in Sweden, and I came here in January 2005.

"I live here now, in a farm cottage, and I feel so welcome. When I work in Sweden, they weren't very strict but they were not so friendly. Here I feel that if you work hard, you're doing a good job and you're happy, then your boss is happy too."

Andrejus fitted in very quickly as, as he said, became part of the family. Certainly, he was something close to a big brother to Harvey (born in 1988) and Tina (born 1990), the two children from my second marriage (to Veronica, AKA Ronni) and he would willingly babysit

The Piggery

them while Ronni and I went out for the evening. I think he missed his own children and eventually they joined him in England. Both have gone on to be very academically successful and have good jobs in the UK. Andrejus brought his new partner over from Lithuania in 2006 and she quickly found work in the Chesham area. She is now a talented gardener and florist - and to think that all this came from one man cycling from London to Chesham!

"Coming here completely changed my life," Andrejus says. " If I'd stayed in Lithuania I would never reach what I've got now. Never. And my children would not have had the same opportunities. In Lithuania, if you have a dad or a mum or an uncle who has a high rank in any job, you're OK - you'll get a job. But if you don't then it's hard and that's not right. Here in England, if you're good enough to do the job you always be very welcome."

In the mid 1990s I decided that some of the older buildings dotted around the farm were in need of repair and renovation, not least the pigstys situated just beyond the front door of Torrington Cottage. The old wooden piggery had suffered significant damage in the Great Storm of autumn 1987 and nothing much had happened to it since, largely because of the fact that we

Anniversary dinner, 1996, Dick Mash on left

131

Farmer ①Tony Harman addresses the gathering
②Stephen Adlington ③Christina Adlington and ④George Piggin

Jack Thurston ④on his golden wedding anniversary – holding the record for being the
furthest from his wife in Australia.
①Sue Sims ②Doug Mash ③Veronica Mash ④Jack Thurston ⑤Irene Snowdon
⑥Chris Tattersell ⑦Marcelle Tattersell ⑧Ron Peters ⑨Pauline Peters ⑩Dan Sims

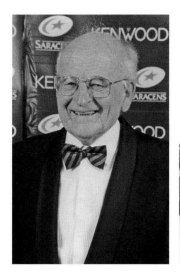

Jack Thurston

①*Alan Lennon* ②*Fred Plumbly* ③*Chris Brown* ④*Roger Randall* ⑤*Antonia Theoday* ⑥*David Burgin*

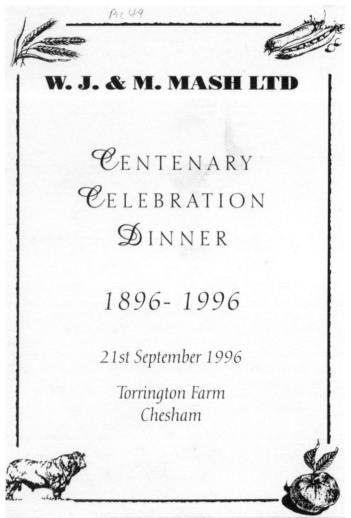

Pic 49

W. J. & M. MASH LTD

Centenary

Celebration

Dinner

1896- 1996

21st September 1996

Torrington Farm
Chesham

didn't keep pigs and had no plans in that direction. At the time I decided to re-build it our business had a good source of income from the tipping that was taking place at Bovingdon Airfield and I felt this money should be reinvested in the farm. So with the help of local builder Allan Hewitt we took down what was left of the piggery and created a brand new building in keeping with the rest of the farm that would serve as a function space for family, friends and paying customers who might want to use its large main hall for events and parties, and a nice place that the family could gather at Christmas and enjoy dinner together.

In all, the work took about six months and I was very pleased indeed with the result. We installed a fully-functioning kitchen and created a conservatory-style extension into the adjoining field so that more guests could be accommodated if required. It was originally built as a single story but there was so much space in the loft we decided to put stairs in and access that, creating a little guest bedroom on one end of the building. We called it The Piggery, and its very first function was a large dinner hosted by the Mash family on September 21, 1996, to celebrate 100 years since the purchase of the farm, and the subsequent development of the family business into a major local concern.

This was truly a spectacular occasion. We invited 400 people, all of whom were in some way connected with WJ&M.Mash Ltd. Guests included family, friends, current and ex-employees, contractors, suppliers and neighbours, and people arrived from far and wide. My uncle, Jack

Mash, gave the welcome and said Grace, then it was on to dinner - not surprisingly, a fine roast sirloin of our own beef! After the meal, our farmer-neighbour Tony Harman proposed a toast to 'the health of the Mash family', followed by a speech from my father, then aged 76. This is worth quoting in full, not least because it helps to put in perspective what had been achieved at Torrington Farm over the century. Also, it seems to pass on the baton from one generation to the next:

"We are pleased to see so many of our family, staff, traders and friends with us tonight, and I hope you have all had some pleasure knowing the Mash family. I would like to pay tribute to our staff past and present, and we have with us tonight six who have given over 50 years of loyal service and friendship. Four are still active with the firm.

"When grandfather H.J. Mash bought Torrington and Wooden Babylon it was vastly different than it is today. The site was cleared and Orchard Leigh House was built. Grandfather lived there for a short while and the late verger of Chesham Church said he remembered the kindly man when he delivered papers. When Grandpa left it was let to Dr Leigh's Health Home and Sun Baths; there was no lack of volunteers to pick the cherries the other side of the fence or push the knots out of the wooden fence to get a better view of the sunbathers! Dr Leigh left to take Champneys to continue his work.

"Gradually, more land was purchased and a new type of farm was built at Lye Green to accommodate horses, pigs and cows. Cottages were built to house the growing staff and over 40 dwellings have been built or altered.

"The farm at the beginning was fruit and vegetables which were sent to London for use in the family business which catered for the railway companies, hotels and later shipping companies. My father, Martin Mash, said as a young man he went to Buckingham Palace to collect orders.

"The produce was taken to London by horse and wagon, followed by steam tractors then solid-tyre Thorneycroft lorries. On the return journey clinker from the boilers and manure from the stables were brought home. The clinker was used to help build the Chesham-Bovingdon road from Rushmoor to Chapel Corner, implemented by stone-picking by the women in winter. The old road came down Grove Lane through Whelpley Hill.

"As the farm progressed a milk round was started. Pigs were sent to the bacon factory and cattle to Tring market or the local butcher's. Corn was also grown and sent to Meads Mill at Tring. During the two wars produce was grown at record levels and in the last war Father would have been Food Controller for the district if the invasion had taken place.

"Orchard Leigh was sold to the Adlington family to become Chesham Preparatory School and has now expanded into a fine school.

Left to right; Doug Mash, Harvey Mash and Dick Mash

"We lost part of Whelpley Ash Farm when it became Bovingdon Aerodrome and we had to re-purchase it with the concrete and buildings. Since then it has brought us mixed blessings; headaches and some rewards. We are pleased to see the market going well and enjoyed by thousands of people.

"Our family has been active in local affairs. Both my father and Jack were captain of Chesham Cricket Club and father, with others, was responsible for the purchase of the football ground. Will Mash was a benefactor of the bowling. Bill Mash was chairman of Ashley Green Parish Council, served on the Curtis Trust and was a Governor of Ley Hill School. I was a founder member of Chesham Boys' Club, held many positions in the N.F.U, the Rabbit Clearance Society and was a Trustee of Chesham Prep School. I housed the Chesham High School Pony Club and let the Ashley Green playing field and pavilion.

"Janet, my wife, still organises the St John Ambulance Medical Comforts Depot after taking over from the late Miss Wheeler in 1970. Douglas has been active in the Young Farmers and local cricket, and is now the chairman of the East Midlands Limousin Society and is a council member. Jane (Bill's daughter) has been very active in Ealing in the church and is secretary to the Alms Houses. She has been responsible for their refurbishment and she has organised, with Douglas, the party tonight, and I thank them for their hard work.

"During the last year Douglas has had a very fine run of successes at the County Show, and two Firsts at the Royal summed up the hard work he and the staff have put in for many years.

"We would like to thank all the services industries for their support. Without them life would be very difficult. I hope you all have a very pleasant evening and enjoy old comrades. Thank you all for coming, and for your friendship."

So many people attended this event that we had to hire a marquee to extend beyond the back of The Piggery and into the field. Friendships old and new were rekindled, and I know for a fact that Susan Bayley enjoyed meeting relatives so much that she started researching the family tree - and where would this book be without her extensive research!? The evening concluded with a spectacular firework display which marked 100 years at Torrington and as the rockets lit up the sky we toasted what had gone before, and what was to come.

And what did come next? For me, sadly, it was divorce from Veronica in 2000. I think it's fair to say that while I've been successful in farming, showing cattle and business in general, success in relationships has eluded me somewhat. I've a feeling it's something to do with my upbringing; certainly, being sent away to school at an early age and being separated from my family made me very independent in some ways and vulnerable in others. That's not always easy to live with, unfortunately, and after two failed marriages I haven't felt the need to enter into a third. But never say never!

In 1999 my Uncle Bill died. As a Board member of W.J. & M.Mash Ltd he was obliged to attend meetings but prior to his death he had a stroke and was unable to carry this out. So to maintain equal numbers on the Board (which then comprised Bill, my father, Bill's daughter Jane and myself) we co-opted Jane's husband, Roger Foster-Smith, on to the board.

Not long after my father became ill and, as with Bill, he was unable to attend board meetings so my sister, Rosemary, was co-opted on to the board. There then followed the kind of family dispute which can arise in a situation where large amounts of money are at stake. In a book such as this, which is meant to be a celebration of a family and a way of life, there is little point in describing the dispute in detail. Suffice to say that it left a trail of bitterness and broken family ties which led to my mother coming on to the Board and, eventually, my sister being cut out of my mother's Will. My opinion is that if certain things had been done properly and openly we wouldn't be in the situation we are in today. Unfortunately, we are and we all have to live with the consequences of it.

My father died in April 2001 and, as was his wish, was buried in Ashley Green Cemetery following a packed funeral at St John's Church, Ashley Green. During the service, which included the traditional Harvest Festival hymn 'We Plough The Fields And Scatter', an address was given by Julia (known in the family as 'Tookey'), one of my father's six grandchildren (along with Katie, Chantal, Michelle, Harvey and Tina). She said this:

"He was one of the best grandfathers anyone could have wished for. He was kind-hearted, generous, warm and exceptionally fun-loving. He was a man who loved his family, the countryside and his television - we all felt for Granny on a Saturday afternoon - but he especially loved his garden.

"I personally will always remember him battling the weather on a Sunday night to go to his garage to find me a bag of potatoes, a few leeks and a cabbage to take back to London. I was probably the only student eating home-grown fresh produce.

"Not only was he incredibly kind, but he had a great sense of humour and loved to do a bit of stirring and when asked a question would never give you an answer. His humour has been filtered down to his great-grandson Harry who, whenever we mention Pop's name, shouts, 'Up The Irish!'

"We all have numerous endearing stories about this well-loved husband, father and grandfather but I don't think any words could describe how much he will be missed by us all today, and always but certainly never forgotten. We are just proud to have called this man 'Pop.'"

A fitting tribute indeed.

Following father's death the farm business was now a partnership between me, my mother,

Henry Mash Court

Jane and Roger. Although Jane was a proud member of the Mash family she wasn't much interested in farming and while Roger had a bit more enthusiasm it wasn't really enough for things to continue as they were. So I offered to buy them both out of the business for a large sum, along with three vacant farm properties which were connected to their side of the family, and they agreed. As it was a significant figure, we agreed that it could be paid out over four years.

During this period - and as I've mentioned with reference to The Piggery, above - I was keen to re-develop some of the farm properties and buildings that had fallen into disrepair. Another of these was the old dairy at Lye Green Farm which over the years had fallen into disuse (for milk production, at least). Tim Stockdale, the international show-jumping champion, had used the land and buildings for some years but he'd decided to move to Northamptonshire and so the buildings would be redundant again. So after the usual long round of consultations and meetings we managed to get planning permission to convert the buildings into seven separate dwellings

Harvey Mash and his pigs

constructed around a courtyard. These comprised two 4-bed, two 3-bed and three 2-bed dwellings, built to a very high specification by Allan Hewitt. Offers to buy these plots came in quickly once building work was started and in 2008 we were very pleased to announce the completion of Henry Mash Court, named after the Victorian gentleman who helped a lady pull her cart out of a ditch and afterwards founded the Mash family business. All the seven houses are named after the seven farms.

The money earned from the sale of Henry Mash Court helped the farm to pay out Roger and Jane, as agreed. My mother and I now held all the shares and Roger and Jane were very happy that they were able to do whatever they liked with a substantial amount of money. That bright future was cut tragically short when Jane died suddenly just a few years later. Roger subsequently moved to New Zealand and settled in Christchurch, where he still lives.

Shortly after my father died my mother was burgled at Woodside, the property we regarded as the family home. The experience shook her up considerably and she decided she no longer wanted to stay there. She moved to a cottage in Grove Lane, right next to the farm, and there she remained until she died in October 2008. In her will she left her shares in the business to me and

Janet and Dick Mash at the Suffolk Show

Harvey, who was by then showing a keen interest in the family business so to that extent it made sense. When she died she left her cottage to Harvey, and that's where he lives today.

The deaths of my parents was the end of an era stretching back before the Second World War, and the changes they saw on the land and in the business were incredible. My father ran the farm, of course, but Mother took an equally keen interest too and when I took over they were always useful sources of advice should I need it. I wish Father had lived a little longer and seen the benefits of the money I invested in the farm from the proceeds of the Limousin cattle. Had he done soon he might have realised that shelling out a lot of money upfront to establish the Brockhurst Herd wasn't such a daft idea after all! Still, whatever he thought of my plan he let me get on with it and I respected him for that.

CHAPTER 13

A Land Down Under

Earlier in the book I mentioned that in the early 1970s I took a trip to New Zealand and en route visited the Perth home of a friend of mine, Greg Thurston, to meet his parents. The warmth of their reception and the country itself impressed me very much and from then on visits to Australia became an integral part of my life.

The Australians and British expats I've met during my long love affair with the country have become some of my best friends. In fact, I'd go as far as to say that I consider them as family now. In 2000 I consolidated my enjoyment of the Australian way of life by buying a piece of land close to Hillary's Boatyard, a coastal suburb of Perth, and building a four-bedroom house on it. Almost every year since I have spent several months there, usually during the British winter which, as a farmer compelled to spend most of my life outdoors, I absolutely hate!

As with The Piggery and Henry Mash Court, I asked local builder Allan Hewitt to carry out the construction work. Greg had a look at the architectural aspects of it in relation to its position;

Allan Hewitt building Doug Mash's house in Hilary Boatyard, Western Australia

Chris Thurston and Allan Hewitt

i.e.in a warm climate and directly facing the Indian Ocean. During the planning stage I had the idea of using bricks from the Bovingdon Brickworks. As this company used part of our land to extract the clay which went into the making of the bricks I thought it would be a nice touch to 'keep it local'. However, there were a few problems with this idea, as Allan explains:

"We went out in the June of 1999 to meet up with the builder we'd employed out there to make sure we were compliant with all the local building regulations. Doug had this idea of using Bovingdon Brick so I packed some samples in my suitcase to show the builder and the architect.

"I got to Customs in Perth and I was in a quandary. I'd read the declaration form and I thought, 'I think I should probably declare a suitcase full of bricks'! So I got in the queue and when it came to my turn the Customs guy picked up my case and said, 'That's heavy, what've you got in there, bricks?' I laughed and the guy asked me what was funny. So I said, 'That's exactly what I've got in the case'. He started questioning me and I asked him did he want to see them. At first he said 'no' but then he seemed quite intrigued and they were brought out, to amusement all round. I think they'd be considered an offensive weapons these days!

"As it turned out the Bovingdon Brick idea wasn't really a goer. The cost of transporting them across the world, plus the Customs duty payable and the fact that they might not be able to withstand the ocean climate made it a non-starter. Plus, they were a completely different size to Australian bricks, which meant that everything would have to be re-set and re-drawn to accommodate them. The builder and the architect weren't happy at all about that!

"Permission for the work to begin came in December 1999 and there were certainly a few challenges, not least getting used to situations which might not affect a house in the UK, like having to install a termite barrier on your damp course! Working in the heat of an Australian summer was an issue too; I'd never experienced anything like it and it could become exhausting. And when it rained, it really rained. I remember being caught in one huge downpour during which 95mm of rain fell in two hours. It was certainly one of the more memorable projects I've worked on!"

The house was completed towards the end of 2000 and I was delighted by it. Finally, after years being accommodated by friends during my trips to Australia, I had a place I could call home. It was a great place to host family and friends visiting from England and my two younger children particularly enjoyed the sunny climate and beach life.

Greg Thurston was delighted (I think!) by my decision to build the house and spend more time Down Under, though he probably dreaded the increased number of nights out he'd have to endure with me! Below, Greg tells the story of how we met:

Doug's house, Australia

"We became friends in 1974 while we were both playing hockey in Chalfont. I'd just got married to my first wife and I was working in a warehouse in Slough. We always intended to come back to Perth and when we did Doug really helped us out with his shipping connections because we had a lot of stuff to transport home. He organised a huge tea chest, which we packed with our stuff before driving it to Southampton and loading it on a ship bound for Fremantle. The ship arrived back in Australia so we went down to the docks in Fremantle to find the tea chest. But there'd been a dockers' strike and it turned out the ship had gone on to Sydney - with all our stuff! Eventually it was found and it came back on the train from Sydney to Perth.

"I'd told Doug that when he visited New Zealand he should stop off and meet my parents, which he did. He got on with them extremely well, particularly my father, Jack, and the two became very close. Doug was also intrigued by the fact that the WACA (the Western Australia Cricket Association) ground which hosted Test matches wasn't too far away from where my mum and dad lived, so that was a big draw for him.

"Over the years we've had many, many Saturday nights out together and a lot of fun. I could have died laughing when he brought over the Bovingdon Bricks in the suitcase! We've been to the cricket together, played golf, had barbecues and parties - when he's over there's always something going on. And of course we've all been back over to Torrington many times and enjoyed his hospitality. He's very much that kind of guy - very close to his friends and always willing to make sure they're having a good time."

Steve Aston my former brother-in-law from my marriage to his sister Joan moved to Sydney in the 1970s and as a family we stayed with him on holiday towards the end of that decade. He has a great story from that time:

"Doug and Joan came over for six weeks. They had Chantal and I think Joan was pregnant with Michelle at the time. They'd had a good holiday, seen all the sights and on the final day we agreed we'd take them to the airport.

"As you do, I asked him if he'd got everything - tickets, passports, money. 'Yep,' he said, 'everything is sorted.' I asked him if he'd phoned up the airport in advance to confirm the booking, which is what you needed to do back then.

"'No,' he said, 'it's all fine, my travel agent has dealt with all that.' I said it was really important to make sure it was done, because flight times could change so quickly but he reassured me that everything was OK so we set off for the airport and along the airport road we spot a Qantas jumbo jet taxi-ing up the runway. In those days you might only have a couple of big international flights per day and I said, 'I hate to tell you this, Doug, but that's your flight about to set off...'

"Well, he wouldn't believe me and we went into the terminal. Sure enough, there was his flight on the board with the word 'Departing' next to it. Doug sees it and tears off like a madman through the airport, pointing his finger in the air and shouting, 'Stop that plane! Stop that plane!'. Needless to say he didn't stop it - the bloody thing had already taken off! - and so they had to fly out the following day.

"Another funny story, which made me laugh a lot, happened a few years later when Doug was divorced from my sister and we'd moved to Western Australia. Doug and I stayed in touch after the divorce, so he came over and asked to stay with us - fine, no problem. We told him that on the Sunday we'd be going to a local market and did he want to come? He said he would, and as he walks out of the door I notice he isn't wearing any footwear. "You'll need something on your feet, mate," I said. "It's 40 degrees out there and the tarmac is boiling."

"Don't worry," he replies, "I'm a farmer. My feet are so hard that it won't bother me."

"Just humour me," I said, "and put on some thongs" (flip-flops). "Nope," he says, "I'm fine."

"OK, so Doug knows best. We arrive in the car park and the surface is so hot you could fry an egg on it. Out we get, and within seconds Doug is running like crazy towards a chip paper he's spotted on the ground, which he stands on like a castaway on a very small desert island. 'Help me, Steve!' he's shouting, 'bring the car back up here!'

'What happened to the farmer's feet?' I laughed.

'Don't mess around,' he shouted, 'do something! My feet are burning into the pavement!'

'I don't know why you don't listen to someone who lives here,' I said, throwing him a spare pair of thongs!"

I think I might still bear the scars from that particular trip to the market! And yes, now I'm seasoned in the Australia climate I'm much more careful than I was, though occasionally I still have my moments. I first met dear friends Don and Elsie Booth during one of those moments. I was lying on Sorrento Beach (not far from my house) and probably hadn't bothered to put sunblock on. As I stretched out, a male voice passing by commented, 'Only a Pom could do something like that…' I looked up to see a middle aged man smiling broadly at me. We got chatting and he introduced himself as Don Booth, a farmer from a small town called Wongan Hills. He and Elsie were staying at a holiday resort nearby and when we got talking we realised we had a lot in common. Sadly, Don died in 2009 but Elsie lives on and whenever I'm over we always spend some time together.

Elsie Booth: "My husband was a cheeky bugger, and so is Doug so they hit it off immediately. Don was the life and soul of the party, just as Doug is. The friendship we had has lasted all these years and we've been to England several times to visit Doug and see what life is like on an English farm. Doug enjoys coming up to visit me because although I don't live on the farm now it's still

Dan and Elsie Booth

in the family so we go up there and he takes an interest in what's going on up there. Then he'll take me back down to his house and I've been invited to all his parties. He definitely hosts the best parties!"

I've had a couple of significant birthdays while out in Australia and yes, I've made the most of them! They usually last a full weekend, with a street party one night, a boat trip down the Swan River in Perth the next day and a golf match or a fishing trip on the final day. Needless to say, quite a lot of drink is involved but I'm a big believer in celebrating the things which need to be celebrated and I love a party. My next-door neighbours in Australia, Denis and Anita Ward, have been to a couple of my parties:

Anita: "The parties brings the street together and get people talking. Day to day, you don't always get to know who your neighbours are but because of his parties he brings out people who might otherwise be strangers."

Denis: "He's adamant we should have a lot of parties. He's a connector of people. He insists on inviting everybody and he gets them all dancing and enjoying themselves. He likes to see people having a good time.

"We first met him in 2006. We'd just moved in and were out the back and this head came over the wall and this voice said, 'Hello, which one's the Principal?' And I said, 'I'm a teacher, not a Principal!' He knew that a Principal had just moved in somewhere on the street and had got confused. That's why he was being cheeky! We didn't see much of him after that as he was going back to England the following day, but when he returned the following year he called in and we became very good friends. We've been over there, staying at the farm.

Anita: "He's always asking us to different things, like joining him at the WACA for the cricket, and sometimes we say no because we don't want to feel we're taking advantage of him. He would do anything for you and I always want to repay him somehow. Doug has said that if we ever left the street, he would go too. And I thought that was a lovely compliment. He's very sweet."

Geoff Thurston (Greg's brother): "Doug's birthdays out here are legendary. He gets a whole load of friends out from England, organises accommodation for everyone and we all just have a great time. He hires a boat and we leave Perth and cruise to Fremantle. He will go to the bridge and say to the captain, 'Can you make it another couple of hours?'! And in recent years there's been the Don Booth Memorial Golf competition between the Aussies and the Poms...."

Ah yes, the Don Booth Trophy. This has been played for twice now now in Don's memory and at the moment the score is 1-1. The Poms, mainly from Chiltern Forest Golf Club, took the trophy from the Aussies last time round and to say we were delighted is a bit of an understatement.

Greg: "The first time was pretty close but in the end we beat them easily so we went over to England in 2016 and they whipped us. I've never seen Doug look so pleased! But there's always a next time...."

One of the most interesting connections I've made in Australia is with a lady called Sue Carrington, her sister Robin and their husbands. By incredible coincidence it turns out that Sue and Robin are the granddaughters of May Brown, daughter of Harry and Lucy Brown - the couple who became friends with HJ Mash 1st and eventually lived in both Torrington Cottage and Torrington House. May Brown married a Welshman, George Jones, and they emigrated to Western Australia in 1927. May was born at Torrington and while Sue, Robin and I are not related by blood there is a family tie through the marriage of a great-aunt (theirs) and a great uncle (mine). Anyway, I simply refer to them as my cousins and that seems the easiest way to describe it. Sue and Robin can take up the story from here:

Sue: "Our great grandparents rented Torrington House from the Mashes and our grandmother May was the youngest of 13 and was born there. She met our grandfather George Jones through the farm. Granddad's family was in the markets business and they bought fruit

A Land Down Under

Poms win back trophy from their Aussie opponents

GOLF

DOUG Mash's team of poms from Chiltern Forest Golf Club won back the Don Booth Trophy from their Australian pals from Perth last week.

Booth was a friend of Mash before passing away and the trophy has been played for twice in his memory, both times in Australia. Having lost the last meeting last year, and now being on home soil, Mash's men were up for the battle and won by three to a half.

Also in the English team were Andy Coyle, Harvey Mash, Colin Grey, Fred Newton, Paul Barratt, Paul Killingley and Chris Wilson, while representing the Aussies were Pete Martin, Geoff Thurston, Greg Thurston, Terry Cameron, Brent Carrington, Rob Brown, Jeff Smith and Brian Addy.

and veg from the Mash family. Granddad was a gambler and they lost all their money, so when our grandmother was about two they decided to start anew and came out by ship in 1927 and arrived in Albany.

"The reason they came there was that grandfather's family had land at Lake Grace. Granddad was granted land in Manjimup if he would grow tobacco and so that's what he did. They had a good life out there and our mother, Marjorie Jones, was one of their offspring. She was always good at keeping in contact with friends and relatives in England via letter and in 1970 I made contact with some of these people when I went out to England and worked in London for 13 weeks. I even stayed in Torrington Cottage! I was aware of Doug then but didn't really know him until we met him properly through our mutual second cousin, Liz D'Arcy Evans."

Robin: "We were there (in England) in 1984 and we got all the rellies together. I'm not sure Doug was around that evening but he must have heard about it because then next time he was in Perth he dropped by to see us. And from there we established this great kinship. It was so strange - Sue and I knew Greg Thurston and his friends from way back when we were teenagers, so we had that connection even before we knew Doug. It took a while to work out that we weren't actual cousins but although there isn't a blood relationship there is a very close one."

Sue: "Doug has always been happy and comfortable out here in Australia. He loves the weather and now he has the opportunity to come out when it suits him. Doug being Doug he has met some of our friends and become friends with them. He's a larrikin (an Australian term for a mischievous person) for sure, but he has a genuine love of people, he's generous to a fault and it's because of Doug that we have this strong relationship with him. We always look forward to him arriving and hearing what he's been up to, and Christmases wouldn't be the same without him here!"

Another family connection in Australia is with Jason Kimber, the nephew of family tree expert Susan Kimber and great-grandson of WJP Mash. He was brought up in Liverpool (where his grandfather John Edward Kimber helped to run the ships' supplies business) and moved to the Isle of Man in his early 20s, where he served as a police officer. In 2007 he answered a recruitment advert for officers to join the Western Australia police force and he came out to live near Perth with his wife and two sons.

ARE INVITED TO CELEBRATE
DOUG'S 70TH BIRTHDAY

AT AN EVENING DINNER DANCE CRUISE
ON THE SWAN RIVER,
PERTH, WESTERN AUSTRALIA
ON SATURDAY 14TH FEBRUARY, 2015
AT 6PM

ALSO, SATURDAY 7TH FEBRUARY
MEET THE POMMIES NIGHT!
SNAGGERS, TINNIES AND DANCING UNDER THE STARS
TO 'NEARLY FAMOUS'
AT 27 QUAYSIDE MEWS, THE BOARDWALK,
HILLARYS, WA6025

Jason: "We saw quite a bit of Doug as kids because we'd come to visit relatives in Chesham most Easters and Christmases. We'd always go along to the farm and have a look at the cows and the horses and we were close to Uncle Dick and Auntie Janet, Doug's parents. Our mother, Sybil, got on particularly well with them.

"As we got older our visits tailed off naturally, but when I was at university in London I used to make time to go up to Chesham and see the family. I always got on well with Doug, he's a larrikin and a loveable rogue. He's very generous and I think a lot of him, particularly because he kept up the contact when we moved to Australia and would visit us regularly. Eventually I worked at the police station in Hillarys, close to Doug's home, so when he was around I'd drop by and see how he was doing.

"He's a joker and a prankster, and he throws great parties. The police were called to one of them after a complaint about noise and I was in the embarrassing position of seeing my colleagues from Hillarys turn up! I think I'm right in thinking that was the time Doug asked one of the female officers if she wanted to dance! Anyway, it was all taken in good spirit and the party went on - but probably a little more quietly…."

Finally, the Mash connection in Australia is complete now that my daughter, Tina, has settled there. She and Harvey always loved to go over for holidays when they were little and I think those experiences stuck in Tina's mind. She's working as a graphic designer in the Perth area and loves the outdoor lifestyle when she's not working. It's great to be able to see her regularly whenever I go over.

Australia is a special place for me and, increasingly, it's where I'm happiest. Would I move out there permanently? I'm still in two minds about that one but I must admit that the place has a big draw for me. So many good friends are there; people I've known for years and whose company I enjoy. That said, there are a lot of those kind of people in England too, so it's probably too difficult to decide!

CHAPTER 14

To the Future

It has been an amazing experience to have witnessed so many massive changes that have taken place in agriculture in my lifetime; from working with horses and the employment of steam through to the early tractors and on to today's highly sophisticated machines.

Being old fashioned, it has been difficult for me to accept the way the modern generation of farmers do things. For example, I was always taught to do good cultivations of the land before seed was planted, rather than today's method of drilling the seed straight into either uncultivated land, or a one pass cultivation in order to grow a good crop of anything. I remain to be convinced what they are all doing is right.

Over many years farming here at Torrington has thrown up many challenges, not least the weather which I am convinced has changed over the last 50-odd years. Also, numerous governments have interfered in how and what we farm, with more recent introductions of single farm payments leading to such things as set aside four crop rules etc. Nevertheless, even through these challenges farming has been and remains enjoyable.

The success of our business, like most successful businesses, is down to having great staff and we have had exactly that over many generations here. That said, I doubt whether in the future many will be able to claim to have worked here for 50 years, unlike previous generations. For one thing, the numbers employed here now are a fraction of what they were years ago; nonetheless the commitment to the cause from the present generation is just as good. One of my lasting memories is of listening to a gang of men in the orchards and all their banter - great times.

The modern generation have been brought up in a totally different world, involving completely different ways of doing things. For example, one of many changes is the way business is now done on farms, leading to the loss of agricultural reps calling by to discuss buying corn, or selling fertilizer or chemicals over a cup of tea or a pint down the pub. In the old days reps would all arrive at 3pm in the packing shed because that was tea time. The modern way is to carry out that business over the mobile phone or the computer to see where the best prices for corn or fertilizer are to be found; quite a different scenario of doing business, and for me not nearly as enjoyable! I have been very fortunate to have had the same grain rep for 40 years namely Austin Clanachan (known as 'Clackers'). Nothing has been more enjoyable than going down to the pub with him for lunch and having a few beers, then agreeing on a price for the next harvest grain. It was important to know where the grain was going and to know you were going to get paid for it, rather than chase the highest price. I have always been happy with the service we got from Clackers; if there were any problems with grain at the delivery point you knew he would sort it out - that was worth a lot to me.

Our conversations over the years were not always confined to agriculture. Football always reared its head and often the trials and tribulations of our private lives would be discussed and joked about. His is a truly great friendship to be treasured.

One of the problems with growing old is not being able to do the things one enjoyed in the past. One of my passions was participating in sport, especially hockey and cricket. This is where I met a lot of my friends. Having retired, the next best thing was watching sport – not only in this country, but all over the world – especially cricket. With Alistair Cook's retirement, this might help my bank balance with flights and beer, but I will miss him around the overseas grounds, scoring all those runs. Well done, especially against the Aussies, and for giving me some ammunition to bait Jack Thurston! Some of the other great times were spent in the box at Watford FC watching football on Saturdays, and Saracens Rugby on Sundays with great friends, whereupon our behaviour with the young waitresses was often unacceptable! The caterers drafted in a very strict lady in the person of Mo Hawthorn. She turned out to be a real diamond in every way; she was a bundle of fun and became a great friend to us all, and she will always have a place in my heart. More recently, great enjoyment has come with following Northants cricket, where Brockhurst Limousin have helped sponsor their 20-20 kit, and seeing them win the 2016 competition. We had the honour of taking our top cow calf Heavenly to the ground, with the groundsmen's agreement, and had our photograph taken along with the victorious team to much amusement. Hopefully sport will give me many more happy times in the future.

Another great rep and friend is Andy Hall, who dealt with chemicals and fertilizer. I've known Andy a similar amount of time as Clackers. He has been a better traveller than Clacks (for a start, he is not Scottish!), having come to Australia on many occasions, especially when England were in Perth playing cricket. Andy, I just wish we could have taken Clackers down to the casino! One other rep I would like to mention is dear old 'Whiskers', from George Brown's. I have known him as long as the others and we have had some great moments together when it has been possible for him to stop earning money for Chris Brown and doing jobs for Janet in the parish. Just order your next air ticket, Pete! To those three and many others, it has been a pleasure doing business with you all.

One of my personal delights over the years has been the management of farming operations especially organising the cattle breeding programme. It was always very satisfying selecting a certain bull to use on a certain cow and having the satisfaction of watching the offspring grow and mature into animals good enough to enter the showring and very occasionally win. Having bred the animal, it was time to select the jockey and five stand out. In the early days it was Colin Souter, who later went on to be the sire of two of my grandchildren, Isla and Finlay, both of whom show great promise in the cattle rings. Colin has one other great attribute: he is cheap around the bars at shows, which is more than I can say for the others! The next stockman who showed the cattle for us was Paul Walker, another very good operator whose expertise in the preparation of cattle helped us have the honour of winning the Limousin Championship at one of the last Royal Shows with no other than Ronick McAinsi. The trophy, along with others, was donated by the Beeney family from Kent. It is such a pity that the Royal Show had to close, along with that of the Smithfield Fatstock Show.

It was around that time that another important venue closed, namely Banbury Mart. This was an important market for the Limousin Society, and when it closed we all lost a new and well-equipped pedigree ring with fine seating and facilities. It was a great loss to the south of the country and once it closed the council of the Limousin Society decided that a sale centre down

Mark Clifford combining winter barley

in the south was not required. So all major sales moved north, and I am sure this has led to many pedigree herds in the south dispersing. Still, I hope we will carry on promoting the breed and it must be said that the sale centre at Carlisle, operated by Harrison and Hetherington, has been very successful for the breed under the guidance of David Tomlinson – which is more than I can say for his football team! I am indebted to the expertise of David, and that of Heather Pritchard, when they have officiated at our sales here at Torrington - thank you both. I am sorry you are so far away, because travelling the lengths of the M1 and M6 is a nightmare.

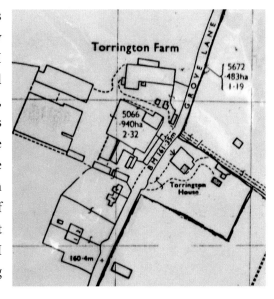

One concern of mine regarding the breed is how much the confirmation of the animals has changed over the last 30 years. I feel we are putting at risk one of the main attributes of the breed, namely easy calving, and I do hope that trait will return in future in order that the breed can continue its popularity. Returning to the stockmen or stockwomen we have had the pleasure to work with brings me to Dougie Macbeath and Sara-Jane Jessop. Together we have had some wonderful times under their management of the Brockhurst Limousins, ably supported by Ben Bellow who has since gone on to pastures new. They have won countless trophies for us up and down the country and they are all stars in their own right. Their handling and preparation of the stock is legendary, and on occasions the victory celebrations have led to many a sore head but Dougie's power of recovery is unmatched, even by his good friend Jimmy Macmillan. Here lies the story of the cap one of them would be wearing, and whoever beat the other in the ring would be entitled to wear the cap until the next time they both met in the ring.

I will always remember our first show that we exhibited, in Edenbridge, Surrey. There were only two competitors in the Limousin section, us and Mary Mount, with her uncle Ted Beeney. On that occasion we were second in every class, but it was a great learning curve. When we exhibited at Edenbridge I had two great lads with me in the lorry; Mark Lake, who worked for me for ten years and a very talented lad who moved on to better himself, and Dougal Culverhouse. We all had great fun and it was a springboard for better days in the ring. I still see Mary occasionally at shows. She now lives with Richard Bartle, helping to manage the Dinmore herd of pedigree limousine in Herefordshire.

One other connection I would like to mention in the cattle world is David and Lesley Sapsed, who farm in Hertfordshire. I knew them in Young Farmers some 45 years ago and as they have pedigree Simmental cattle our paths crossed frequently in the early days of showing. Occasionally we would end up together in an interbreed competition final, and if we were lucky enough to beat them Lesley would jokingly say we had beaten them with an imported animal - which may have been the case! Latterly, all our animals have been home-bred and Lesley now says it was the judges' fault!

In recent years one of the things governments have changed is the way you get paid at the scrap yard when delivering scrap. Many years ago, my early flights to Australia were sponsored by the extraction of copper and lead from the disused airfield at Bovingdon. With my good friend Eamonn Thornton I would dig it up at weekends, set fire to it so the lead would run off, then bag it up and take it to the yard the next week and get paid in cash! No doubt Eamonn's money went into his cars (or Mary's handbag!) whereas mine found its way to the local travel

Tina and Harvey Mash

Colin Souter with Finlay

Doug with Katie Wilkinson

Doug with Katie Wilkinson on ostriches – which is the old bird?!

Mo Hawthorn in Australia

David Sapsed's marriage to Lesley in the Hawaiian islands

agent, in the form of Phil Davis, where the notes would help pay for my ticket to Australia. That transaction led to the start of another great friendship and in more recent times Phil has organised my big birthdays in Australia. The first one was my 60th, to which he invited a fellow employee, namely Sarah, to join him over there and that was the catalyst which ignited their romance, leading to them getting married on the Hudson River in New York, a truly magnificent occasion for a lovely couple.

On a more personal note, although I have tried to make a success of farming here at Torrington my private life has not turned out very successfully, with two marriages ending in divorce. I found it very difficult losing the closeness of the children; something I am sure has affected my relationship with them now. Perhaps with my grandchildren it may be better. Even though my marriages didn't work out I have to say I have had some wonderful times with a very special lady, Katie Wilkinson, the sister of David Sapsed. We had some amazing times travelling to wonderful places such as New Zealand, South Africa and Barbados, but the best one would be the Hawaiian Islands for David and Lesley's wedding, a wonderful occasion on the beach. These good times will remain with me forever. Indeed, I would like to thank all those lovely people who have helped make my life here at Torrington so enjoyable.

A few years away from my 70th birthday I decided the time was right to begin the process of handing over the management of Torrington Farm. There was really only one candidate for the job, and luckily his surname is Mash. This is my son, Harvey, who showed a keen interest in farming at an early age, went on to college and university to study agriculture and now shows himself to be a competent and thoughtful farm manager.

The legacy Harvey has inherited from previous generations is a very good one. At the time of writing we own and farm 1,200 acres and we have 250 head of cattle. The work put in by our forebears has resulted in land which is very fertile, bringing us consistently good yields, and there is also the land at Bovingdon Airfield which provides us with additional income through the weekly market and the film-related activities there.

Each generation brings with it new ideas and new ways of managing the land and running the business. I made the difficult decision to grub up the orchards when I took over from Father and Bill and I'm sure they must have wondered if that decision was a good one, given that the Mash business was founded on the growing and supply of fruit and vegetables. As it turned out it was a good decision, as was that to invest in pedigree cattle.

In recent years Harvey and I have differed – sometimes strongly – on how the farm and the Mash business should be managed. These haven't been easy times for either of us; we're both strong-willed people with firm ideas on how things should be. Such is the nature of transition

Mary Beeny with Royal Show trophy

Doug with Harvey and Tina on his 65th birthday

Doug's mother on her 90th birthday helicopter ride

Phil and Sarah Davis

*Grain rep
Austin Clanachan
(Clackers)*

Greg Thurston

between one generation and the next. There were similar disagreements in and around Torrington Farm in the period we've covered in the book, and while the business changed and diversified, it did continue to prosper.

My hope is that Torrington Farm remains in excellent shape for the generations ahead who will inherit it. We live in uncertain times and the future is, as always, unwritten. However, I hope that the knowledge accumulated here since the end of the 19th century will stand us in good stead as we negotiate the decades ahead.

On a personal note, I would like to thank so many people who have contributed towards this book, helping to shed light on the changes the farm and surrounding area have undergone over the last 120 years.

Firstly, a big thank-you must go to Harvey for commissioning this book as a gift to mark my 70th birthday. Since the old safe was opened and the documents, letters and old photos of the farm were discovered, we have puzzled over what to do with this legacy and I'm delighted that it has been preserved in this way.

I'd like to thank the editor, Tom Henry, for the way he has compiled the book. It has been great fun working with him. I would like to thank everyone who has contributed towards the story of the farm; no matter how large or small, they have all been appreciated. Special posthumous thanks must go to Pauline Peters, Josie Puddephatt and Don Dell, who sadly died during the period this book was written.

Another big thank-you must go to my cousin, Susan Kimber, for researching and drafting the Mash family tree. This is a spectacular document that runs to many feet in length and it is a real sight to behold! Thanks, Sue.

I'd also like to thank Peter Hawkes, the eminent Chesham historian and publisher of local books, for his excellent layout and design, and eye for detail. He has been helped by Chris Sims, Keith Fletcher and Sheila Hart.

My final thanks go to you, the reader, for taking the time to read this book. I hope you've enjoyed our story, and have learned something of the changing nature of the British countryside over the last 120 years.

Best wishes,
Doug Mash